**DEMYSTIFYING BUSINESS INTERRUPTION INSURANCE**
A Guide to Contemporary Nigerian Practice

By

# Peter Offiong

B.Sc., M.Sc., AIIN, ACIB, GNIM, ACA

**DEMYSTIFYING BUSINESS INTERRUPTION INSURANCE**
**A Guide to Contemporary Nigerian Practice**


Copyright © Peter Offiong 2020

*All rights reserved. No part of this publication may be reproduced or transmitted, in any form or by any means, electronic, mechanical, photocopying, recording or otherwise, or stored in any retrieval system, without the prior written permission of the author.*

## PREFACE

In the course of advising a client in 2016 to take up a business interruption policy, we exchanged several emails where clarity was sought on several terms and how these concepts could impact claims. The client subsequently requested for a short and simplified write up (not a textbook) which could explain the core of the cover. Whilst putting down a five-page document for the client, the idea of a book that will serve as a guide to clients was conceived.

This book will appeal to buyers of insurance whilst also serving as a refresher to insurance students and practitioners across all arms of the insurance market. The intention is to simplify as much as possible the core concepts at the heart of business interruption underwriting and claims. The book challenges the norms in the Nigerian market whilst drawing on practice and emerging issues in other markets.

As the book was being finalised, Covid-19 (coronavirus) became a topical issue not just in terms of the health emergencies but the interruption caused by the global lockdown. It became necessary to begin a conversation on this uncharted territory in the final chapter of the book. The views expressed in this chapter are therefore not definitive.

## ACKNOWLEDGEMENTS

I received great support from Mr. Bayo Samagbeyi (FASCON) who not only encouraged me to complete the book but was kind enough to review drafts of this book with modesty I found difficult to resent.

I am immensely indebted to a couple of people who assisted me and made useful inputs in the course of writing this book. Of special mention is the management and staff of Scib Nigeria & Co. Ltd led by Mr. Shola Tinubu. They challenged my thought process and made me love insurance broking.

I would like to express my gratitude to members of CSU 1 at Scib, my former students at Old Klass Training Institute, CIIN Lecture Centre, Private Students, and industry friends who had provided useful feedback during our many interactions in the course of writing this book.

Most importantly my loving wife and children (Omowumi, Emediong, and Ekomobong) made the home comfortable enough to play, work and write. I am grateful for your support.

**Peter Offiong**
August 2020

## DEDICATION

In memory of John Offiong whose business of life was interrupted on 2$^{nd}$ November 2012.

## TABLE OF CONTENTS

**Chapter 1: Overview of Business Interruption Insurance...... 1**
1.1 Historical Timelines................................................ 1
1.2 Recent Developments ............................................ 3
1.3 Definition of Terms................................................ 4
1.4 The Relevance of Business Interruption Insurance.......... 6
1.5 Foreign Influence on The Nigerian Practice................. 8
1.6 The Concept of Business Interruption Insurance........... 10

**Chapter 2: Understanding the Essentials of Cover –Part 1..... 21**
2.0 General Introduction............................................... 21
2.1 The Workings of the Bi Policy.................................. 28

**Chapter 3: Understanding the Essentials of Cover- Part 2...... 33**
3.1 Maximum Indemnity Period...................................... 33
3.2. Understanding Variable Cost and the Gross Profit Model.. 37
3.3 Dealing with Inflation............................................. 41
3.4 Computing Gross Profit Sum Insured –Worked Example............................................................. 43

**Chapter 4: Rating the Policy............................................. 47**
4.1 Introduction......................................................... 47
4.2 Rating Considerations 49

**Chapter 5: Policy Design and Extensions –Part 1................... 55**
5.1 Expanding the Core Cover........................................ 55

**Chapter 6: Policy Design and Extensions –Part 2.................. 71**
6.1 Engineering Policies................................................ 71
6.2 Fines & Penalties................................................... 74
6.3 Research & Development......................................... 76
6.4 Outbreak of Notifiable Disease................................. 78
6.5 Attempted Murder/Suicide....................................... 80
6.6 Loss of Licence/Franchise........................................ 81
6.7 Contingency Covers................................................ 84
6.8 Alien Abduction, Etc............................................... 86

**Chapter 7: Clauses Clarifying the Core Cover...................... 87**
7.1 Other Circumstances (Business Circumstances) Clause.... 87
7.2 Alternative Trading Clause....................................... 88
7.3 New Business Clause.............................................. 89
7.4 Professional Accountants Clause............................... 90
7.5 Accounts Designation Clause.................................... 91
7.6 Accumulated Stocks Clause...................................... 92
7.7 Departmental Clause.............................................. 94
7.8 Salvage Sale Clause................................................ 95

**Chapter 8: Claims Management......................................... 99**
8.0 Overview of Business Interruption Claim..................... 99
8.1 Legal and Other Issues to Consider For Claims Presentation:................................................ 100
8.2 Steps to Take Immediately Following A Loss................ 106

**Chapter 9: Claims Management –Worked Examples.............. 113**
9.1 Example 1............................................................. 113
9.2 Example 2............................................................. 117
9.3 Example 3............................................................. 119
9.4 Important Note...................................................... 122
9.5 Practice Question...................................................123

**Chapter 10: Emerging Issues........................................... 125**
10.0 General Overview................................................. 125
10.1 Non Damage Business Interruption............................. 126
10.2 Contingent Business Interruption and Supply Chain......... 127

**Chapter 11: Pandemics (Coronavirus) And Business Interruption............................................... 129**
11.0 General Overview................................................. 129
11.1 Cover Triggers...................................................... 130
11.2 A Few Decided Cases............................................. 133

**Bibliography.............................................................. 139**

## CHAPTER 1:
# OVERVIEW OF BUSINESS INTERRUPTION INSURANCE
## 1.1 HISTORICAL TIMELINES

Business Interruption Insurance as we know it today was a response to the yearnings of merchants and business owners for protection against consequential losses resulting from marine and fire damage. Although there has been little development of business interruption following marine loss, that of fire has witnessed significant development over the years across various continents.

Below are the major global historical timelines:

| | |
|---|---|
| 1797 | First attempts by Minerva Universal (UK) to insure consequential costs and loss of income. |
| 1817 | The *Hamburger Generalfeuerkasse* covers loss of rent as a supplement to fire insurance. |
| 1821 | Time loss policy introduced in England, also known as the per diem method, involving daily/weekly compensation. |
| 1857 | *Chomage* insurance introduced in France, known as *systeme forfaitaire*. The consequential cost from a fire loss is covered by a fixed percentage of the sum insured. |
| 1880 | Dalton, an insurance agent in Boston (US), introduces the expression "use and occupancy", already a familiar concept in fire insurance of the loss of production following fire. |

| | |
|---|---|
| 1899 | The British loss of profits system, where turnover is a key figure, is developed by Ludovig McLlellan from Glasgow, Scotland. |
| 1906 | Business interruption insurance based on the UK model introduced in Sweden. |
| 1910 | Machinery business interruption policy approved in Germany by the supervisory authorities. |
| 1938 | The gross earnings form – also known as the US system introduced in the United States. |
| 1939 | Standard business interruption wordings known as the "standard policy" are drawn up in England and Ireland, forming the basis of what is known as the UK system. |
| 1956 | Independent fire business interruption policy introduced in Germany |
| 1986 | The *ISO* recommends replacing the gross earnings form with the business income coverage form that is frequently used in the US today. |
| 1989/91 | *Association of British Insurers* (ABI) publishes new recommended business interruption wordings. |
| From 2000 | Greater focus on business interruption exposure in response to society's increasing dependency on electronic media (cyber exposures), globalization and the terrorist attack on the World Trade Center. |

NIGERIAN MARKET –

Historical records trace the emergence of modern insurance in Nigeria to 1902 with the appointment of a law firm (Irwing and Bonnar) as Lagos agent by Royal Exchange Company of London. By 1918, this developed into a full agency office and by 1921 became a full branch of Royal Exchange Assurance, London. This company concentrated on Fire Insurance in its early days. Whilst there is no clear evidence as to when the first Consequential Loss/Business Interruption policy was issued in Nigeria, chances are that one may have been issued between 1910 and 1949 due to the various fire incidents in Lagos, the first and second world war as well as the demands of the UK companies operating in Nigeria at the time.

Policies issued in Nigeria post-independence (from 1960) were named Consequential Loss Insurance until very recently when the nomenclature changed to Business Interruption. For simplicity, the phrase "Consequential Loss" and "Business Interruption" will be used interchangeably throughout this book.

## 1.2 RECENT DEVELOPMENTS

Recent conversations around business interruption insurance have been in the areas of supply chain risk, cyber risk and terrorism. Outside Nigeria, new products are being introduced along with many modifications to wordings to simplify business interruption, make it easier to understand and offer greater protection to reflect the changing nature of risk facing organisations. Our environment is emerging and there is a need to catch up with developments in other fields for which insurance is meant to provide protection.

## 1.3 DEFINITION OF TERMS

Before we get carried away with technicalities of the concepts, let us present below a quick definition of terms as may be found in most modern policy documents:

**Revenue**: The money paid or payable to the Insured for services rendered in the course of the Business at the Premises.

**Turnover:** The amount that the business has earned (Sales and Revenue mean the same thing).

**Annual Turnover:** This is income received from the sale of goods or services during the 12 months immediately before the date of claim as per the annual financial statements.

**Standard Turnover:** The turnover generated in those months in the previous year corresponding with the period affected by the Damage.

**Adjusted Standard Turnover:** This is when Standard Turnover is adjusted to reflect any necessary trend such that it then represents the turnover that would have occurred had it not been for the Damage.

**Reduction in Turnover:** Adjusted Standard Turnover less actual turnover generated during the indemnity period.

**Indemnity Period:** The period beginning with the occurrence of the Incident and ending not later than the Maximum Indemnity Period thereafter, during which the results of the business shall be affected in consequence thereof.

**Maximum Indemnity Period:** The period after which BI cover ceases to operate, whether the results of the business continue to be affected or not. It is usually stated on the policy schedule and could typically range from 12 months to 36 months.

**Gross Profit:** The amount by which: i) the sum of the amount of the Turnover and the amounts of the closing stock and work in progress shall exceed ii) the sum of the amounts of the opening stock and work in progress and the amount of the Specified Working Expenses (purchases, carriage, freight, etc.)

**Specified Working Expenses:** These are costs/overheads that the company has assumed will reduce in direct proportion to the reduction in turnover, e.g. purchases, carriage, and freight.

**Rate of Gross Profit:** Gross Profit for the previous 12 months divided by the turnover for the previous 12 months multiplied by 100.

**Increase in Cost of Working:** Additional expenditure (subject to the Specified Working Expenses clause) necessarily and reasonably incurred for the sole purpose of avoiding or diminishing the reduction in Turnover which but for that expenditure would have taken place during the Indemnity Period.

**Additional increased cost of working:** This is a form of cover offered as an extension to a standard business interruption policy that removes the economic limit that would otherwise be applied to the increased cost of working cover. It may be needed by businesses that operate in an extremely competitive environment, whose customers are extremely difficult to regain once lost.

**Advanced Loss of Profits:** This protects the future earnings of a new business or an extension to an existing business. It differs from a standard business interruption policy in that the indemnity period only starts to run from the date on which income would have started to be earned from the new enterprise, rather than the date of the physical damage.

**Average:** This is a penalty for underinsurance. If the sum insured is less than the sum produced by applying the Rate of Gross Profit to the Annual Turnover (or to a proportion of the increased multiple thereof where the Maximum Indemnity Period exceeds 12 months), the amount payable should proportionately be reduced.

**Proportionate Reduction:** A BI term that means the same thing as Average.

**Excess:** The first amount of any claim that the company must bear themselves. The claim payment is made over this amount. It may be a monetary amount or a period.

**Franchise:** If a loss is less than the franchise amount, nothing is paid, but the loss is paid in full if it exceeds the franchise amount. It may be a monetary amount or a period.

**Event**: Damage to Property used by the Insured at the Premises for the purpose of the Business.

**Premises**: Buildings at the address or addresses shown in the Schedule, including their grounds, all within the boundaries for which the Insured are responsible and being unless more specifically described in the Schedule, occupied solely by the Insured for the purpose of the Business.

**Savings:** Saved variable costs that would have been incurred had there not been a loss.

## 1.4 THE RELEVANCE OF BUSINESS INTERRUPTION INSURANCE

Scenario planning may provide a situation as well as an estimate of how long a business can survive without revenue coming in to pay the on-going expenses especially following a major incident such as fire, flood or explosion but no business ever wishes for this. Some business owners or managers completely ignore the possibility of an interruption to the business income flow even though previous experience or those of other businesses suggest otherwise. Disaster experience is certainly not the best teacher! Usually, some businesses only get to appreciate the magnitude of their losses when the unexpected occurs.

In our environment, the tendency is often to attribute disasters to the "will of God" and subsequently cry to the government for assistance. This assistance often would not come despite promises made by politicians. In the end, the business whether small, medium or large scale ends up grappling the lost income following a disaster. Some businesses never recover and it adds to the economic waste and other social issues.

Typically even if the critical assets of an organisation are damaged or destroyed, the business may still have financial obligations to fulfil in terms of bills, salaries, debt servicing, etc. This usually exasperates the situation and could force the owners into bankruptcy depending on the structure of incorporation. By putting in place the appropriate insurance, not only is the value of the asset protected, but the loss of income caused by the damage can also be reimbursed. For example, if a factory is damaged by fire or flood, it might be of immediate comfort that the damaged property will be replaced or reinstated by the insurance company. It is equally important that the income stream to the business derived from the factory is also protected. If there is a Business Interruption Insurance in place, the risk and associated stress following a significant loss will be alleviated from the business.

Using the example of a damaged factory above, Business Interruption Insurance will cover loss of profit from the damage. Additionally, Business Interruption Insurance can, in certain circumstances, provide for loss of profit where the factory is not directly damaged. For example, it can protect from a disruption caused by public utilities, restriction of access, and/or closure by public authority caused by an insured event. Essentially dependencies of the business in terms of suppliers or customers may be protected where the insured event disrupts the business of the suppliers and customers. This means if a supplier or customer has a flood, fire or suffers storm damage and cannot operate, the factory which depends on the input or output of these parties can be protected from a loss of profit.

At the end of the day, it all comes down to this simple question: Do you want to risk your investment and your on-going financial security? As we will get to see in the course of this book, business interruption insurance is that protection that every business needs.

## 1.5 FOREIGN INFLUENCE ON THE NIGERIAN PRACTICE

Like every other thing in Nigeria, there is always a fusion of cross-continental practice so much so that practitioners are sometimes confused as to the right principles at play. Historically, the practice of insurance in Nigeria started during the colonial days largely influenced by UK practice. However, just the same way the Nigerian politicians fell in love with the US presidential system of government; insurance practitioners have also adopted US practices one way or the other. Sometimes these influences have come from global clients who insist on the adoption of their Master Policy wordings.

Whilst a majority of Business Interruption policies in the Nigerian market is tailored to suit UK practice. There are, however, instances where policies are a hybrid of the UK and US practice. The problem with the latter is the difficulty in interpretation at the time of claim. Again, because there is a dearth of interest in this class of insurance, the insurers, loss adjusters, brokers and clients are sometimes left in the dark at the time of claim. Whoever has the highest level of influence gets what they want in most cases. The arguments sometimes are not based on the technicality of policy structure or wordings.

A very basic contrast of the UK and US practice is shown below. Readers who are interested in a deeper understanding of the differences are encouraged to consult further reading materials contained in the bibliography:

### Comparison of UK and US Wordings

| Item | UK | US (ISO) |
|---|---|---|
| Policy | Separate conditions | Appendix to a property policy |

| Scope of cover/insurance protection | Commercial operational readiness | Technical operational readiness. Option: 1 month post indemnity period. Finished stock excluded. |
|---|---|---|
| Loss of market as a result of a loss of income | Covered during indemnity period | Not covered |
| Income at risk/ Insurance value/ sum insured | Gross profit (fixed costs and operational profit) Option: salaries/wages separate. | Business income (fixed costs and operating unit) Option: wage amount separate NB: insured amount dependent on coinsurance percentage. |
| Limitation of liability | Indemnity period usually 12 months. No waiting period in some cases | Coinsurance percentage: no liability period. Standard waiting period: 72 hours |
| Premium calculation/ premium rate | Fire premium rate (contents) multiplied by an adjustment factor | Fire premium rate (building) multiplied by adjustment factor (coinsurance percentage) |
| Premium | Premium rate multiplied by gross profit | Premium rate multiplied by insured amount |
| Indemnity principle | Restore operations as if no loss had occurred | Loss of production during repair time |
| Others | Material damage provision | |

## 1.6 THE CONCEPT OF BUSINESS INTERRUPTION INSURANCE

The main purpose of a Business Interruption policy is to maintain the turnover of the business during the indemnity period following an insured incident so that the company can resume trading/business activities at its anticipated pre-loss trading/activity level subject to the prevailing business circumstances. This means if there is no business to maintain, the policy will not engage. This is why a Business Interruption policy will not engage if a business simply ceases to operate or goes into liquidation.

Conceptually, business interruption insurance covers loss of gross profit and the increased cost of working, during a period of interruption. In reality, the generic nature of the cover, irrespective of whether the insured is a service provider, retailer or manufacturer creates complexities which are often compounded by unclear policy wordings or language. As unclear as it might seem, the starting point must always be the policy wording.

The standard definition of Business Interruption is as follows:

*The words Consequential Loss shall mean loss resulting from interruption of or interference with the Business carried on by the Insured at the Premises in consequence of DAMAGE to property used by the Insured at the Premises for the purposes of the Business.*

We will continue to expand on the above definition by explaining its key elements in the course of this book.

Before we delve into the concepts, we need to be guided by the operative clause of the policy. Like in every other insurance policy, this is the basis on which insurers will consider making any payment in the event of a claim. Since the Nigeria Insurers Association (NIA) have not yet come up with a separate definition, we will adopt the standard All Risks business interruption wording suggested by the Association of British Insurers (ABI) as follows:

*'The insurer agrees (subject to the terms, definitions, exclusions, conditions of this policy) that if after payment of the first premium any building or other property used by the insured at the Premises for the purpose of the Business be accidentally lost, destroyed or damaged during the period of insurance (or any subsequent period for which the insurer accepts a renewal premium) and in consequence the business carried on by the insured at the Premises be interrupted or interfered with then the insurer will pay to the insured in respect of each item in the Schedule the amount of loss resulting from such interruption or interference provided that:*

*1) At the time of the happening of the loss destruction or damage there shall be in force an insurance covering the interest of the insured in the property at the Premises against such loss, destruction or damage and that i) payment should have been made or liability admitted therefor, or ii) payment would have been made or liability admitted thereof but for*

> *the operation of a proviso in such insurance excluding liability for losses below a specified amount.*

2) The liability of the insurer under this policy shall not exceed
   i) in the whole the total sum insured or in respect of any item, its sum insured or any other limit of liability stated in the Schedule at the time of the loss, destruction or damage.
   ii) the sum insured (or limit) remaining after deduction for any other interruption or interference consequent upon loss, destruction or damage occurring during the same period of insurance unless the insurer shall have agreed to reinstate any such sum insured (or limit)."

The concepts earlier mentioned are expounded by the above operative clause. We, therefore, need to be clear regarding the following:

a) The insured. Who is being insured and has the entity been properly and appropriately defined?

b) What are the Premises and has the Business carried out at each site (or elsewhere including clients' locations) been properly identified?

c) Has the Business been properly described? Any failure to identify key aspects of the business at inception can lead to difficulties should a claim be made. Has the substance and legal form of the business been clearly expressed?

d) Has the interest of the insured in relevant physical assets been insured against under a material damage cover and is it meaningful for this concept of material damage proviso to be applied?

## 1.6.1 The Insured

The insured can take different forms ranging from limited liability company, public liability company, partnership, corporation, sole proprietor, joint ventures, corporate groups, etc.
The insured must be clearly and accurately defined. It is also vital to fully identify all the entities that could be affected by

an interruption to the business irrespective of the legal forms they might take. For instance, where part of a business operation may have been incorporated as a limited liability company and part continued to run as partnership confusion can arise as to what costs and income streams properly belong in each part of that operation. The legal form of the documentation might not reflect the economic substance intended by the insured business. Joint Ventures are also another classic example. Depending on the share ownership of the joint venture business, it might not fall within the definition of a subsidiary. For instance NNPC/TOTAL/ELF joint ventures. Many policies are issued in the name of a holding company and/or subsidiary companies and a failure to explicitly include the joint venture operation could lead to a conclusion that it was not part of the insurance programme. Such a conclusion would be more likely where, for example, sums insured were not increased to reflect its existence before the claim occurs.

Another scenario could play out with a group structure when the policy is taken in the name of a business that was once the holding company. With time, the group structure may have become more complex and the initial holding company may have become one of several operating subsidiaries of another entity. If the policy remains in the name of what is now a subsidiary company then technically businesses higher up the group hierarchy, or fellow subsidiaries of such businesses would have no cover. Another interesting twist could occur with limited liability companies whose affairs are piloted by the ruling mind (directors). Certain history of the directors could, therefore, impact on the insured. The disclosure issues for directors of companies or principals of unincorporated businesses are always worth reviewing regularly.

Often policies are arranged on a "group" basis as a loss at one subsidiary could well have a knock-on effect on the profits of another. It is important to note however that any identified Insured must have more than just a financial interest in the business continuing. A bank, for example, has an insurable interest in the property the subject of a loan or mortgage and is frequently noted in a property damage policy as a joint insured. However, a bank cannot be a joint insured on a Business Interruption policy because its own business (banking) will not be the defined *Business* of the Insured. Liability of insurers will therefore not engage.

### 1.6.2 The Business

In the event of a claim, only the business named and activities described will be indemnified. It is therefore important to state all the constituent parts of an insured's business that might be affected by an interruption. If the particular activity is not identified within the definition then the policy may not respond to the losses incurred by that part of the business. There are many complimentary activities that insured businesses can sometimes enter into alongside their core activity. This should be mentioned when incepting the policy. It is always important to disclose all given the extra exposure each activity brings to the insured. For instance, a business might be diversifying into unrelated activities in response to the changing economy. The new aspect of the business might produce income as distinct from the Gross Profit of the business operation from the core activity. There will be a need to ensure that this element of the business is notified to insurers.

A new business operation could constitute an activity sufficiently different from the main business to require formal expansion of the description of the business on the schedule. For instance, a business previously engaged in the importation and packaging of cement exploring the manufacturing and exportation of the same product would be significantly altering their risk profile.

The definition of business could also be affected by the legality and morality of its practice. A business which is presented to insurers should be run in accordance with the law and public policy. This is a cardinal characteristic of an insurable risk.

Brokers are inclined to draft their wordings to give an all-encompassing definition of the business, along the lines of present and future activities undertaken or to be undertaken by the Insured.

The insured owes a duty to the underwriters to keep them fully informed of any unusual or hazardous activities although the majority of the insured's activities are usually a matter of public knowledge freely available from published reports and accounts and articles on their website.

### 1.6.3 The Premises

It is also important to identify all the Premises that might be affected by an interruption. Premises can be expanded to include other premises, not in the Insured's occupation or control, but the initial list needs to include all those that they do occupy.

Just as we saw above with the definition of Business, brokers are often inclined to request an all-embracing definition (subject to separate detailed disclosure) along the lines of any premises owned occupied or utilised by the Insured within the Territorial Limits, which has been declared to and accepted by the Insurers.

There are three general issues to consider under the heading 'Premises'. These are the scope of the cover, the trade conducted at the Premises, and the basis of tenure.

**The Premises- Scope of Cover**
Usually, the scope gets clarified by the terms of the policy as well as custom and usage. For instance, would set back from the public highway or a fairly long road be classified as part of a premises? Would the airspace be seen as the premises and if yes, what height? The term Premises can have a very wide application. Premises embraces, for example, inspection pits set into pave-

ments giving access to underground utilities.

**The Premises -Trade or Business**

It is also important to consider the trade or business at the Premises. There is the concern from a business interruption perspective that focusing the cover on the Premises may not embrace all of the activities of the insured business. The business might be primarily carried out off-site or at multiple clients' locations. This is a very common situation in the construction industry, for auditors, consultants, etc. The Premises defined in the policy provide the base location and administrative support, but the turnover is achieved off-site. Business interruption cover that is only available after Damage occurs at the Premises might be insufficient. Contract Site Extension clause, therefore, becomes very useful in such situations. We must also not forget that some business premises have moved online. Companies whose businesses are carried out either partly or fully online should be so described.

**The Premises -Tenure**

The last point on the Premises must be tenure. Being a tenant increases the business interruption risk. A tenant is likely to have little control over the speed of building repairs following the occurrence of an insured event and consequently is unable to control a mitigation strategy to minimise a business interruption claim in the way that would be possible if the building was owned. However, nothing stops a tenant from a risk management point of view, from discussing with the landlord a protocol for the reinstatement of damage before it occurs. This will afford a lot more control in terms of tenant's ability to insure which will expedite reinstatement in the event of a loss. This will certainly help in the event of a business interruption claim.

**1.6.4 Damage and the Material Damage Proviso**

Usually, the cover granted is a business interruption which flows from damage caused by an insured peril, or in the case of an All Risks policy from an external cause not otherwise excluded.

The material damage proviso is fused with the operative clause in some policies and set out separately in others. A typical material damage proviso might read thus:

*The Operative clause will trigger provided that at the time of the happening of the damage there shall be in force an insurance covering the interest of the insured in the property at the premises against such damage and that payment shall have been made or liability admitted therefore under such insurance.*

The main purpose of the material damage proviso has been to ensure that sufficient funds are available to facilitate reinstatement, which in turn will mitigate the BI loss. The second objective is to avoid the need for the business interruption adjuster to duplicate the work of the material damage adjuster in investigating the cause and considering the application of any clauses precedent to liability.

Merely satisfying the material damage proviso does not mean that the claimed business interruption loss will be covered. The business interruption losses that are being claimed still have to flow from the Damage. Assets which may be loaned by a customer, supplier or joint venture partner are again relevant. There may be no material damage insurance in respect of those items but the business interruption loss that derives therefrom caused by the operation of an insured peril where this has also damaged other property insured by the business is covered. The satisfaction of the proviso does not restrict business interruption losses to merely those that derive directly from Damage to the assets that satisfy the proviso itself. However, the Damage must still be the proximate cause of loss. The situation is different for Non-Damage Business Interruption which will be discussed in a subsequent chapter.

The material damage proviso also has its weakness. The general concern is that when it comes to the availability of sufficient funds to effect reinstatement, the material damage proviso fails. This is because the proviso neither requires adequacy of sums insured nor that insurance should be on a reinstatement basis. The proviso is either satisfied or it is not. The need to anticipate separate material damage and business interruption investigations into causation is old-fashioned given that most modern policies are often combined with even a single deductible!

The material damage proviso was conceived when the various covers were purchased as separate policies. Not only have commercial combined covers become the norm, but also the breadth and availability of BI extensions have increased. The extent to which the traditional material damage proviso wording can be applied to these extensions varies between wordings.

One important BI case which directly deals with material damage proviso occurred in the UK and is that of <u>Glengate - KG Properties Ltd -v- Norwich Union Fire Insurance Society Ltd and Others (1995).</u> Glengate bought an old department store building on Oxford Street to redevelop. It took out two policies with *Norwich Union*, one for material damage and one for business interruption. It had a temporary site office in the building, which was used by the construction professionals, including the architects. There was a fire that destroyed the site office and with it a large number of drawings on which the architects were working. Importantly, the drawings were very clearly the architects' property. They retained the copyright and ownership and the drawings were in their possession. Once completed, *Glengate* was to have a license to use the drawings.

The architects had not insured the drawings. There was an extension in the material damage policy that included temporary offices and plans, but only if these were the 'property of the insured or for which they are responsible'. Norwich Union argued that the material damage proviso in the business interruption policy was not satisfied because there was no cover in force for the drawings. The two majority judgments rejected this argument. These distinguished the type of interest covered by the business interruption policy and the insurable interest necessary to insure property under a material damage policy. It was held that the former was broader and focused on the fact that the business interruption cover clause only required the property to be used by the insured for the purposes of the business at the premises. It did not spell out a need to have a proprietary interest (e.g., ownership). In contrast, they found that the material damage cover required an insurable interest in a more narrow sense, namely a proprietary or contractual interest in the property.

By this reasoning, the Court of Appeal in the UK found that there was sufficient insurable interest to allow the claim under the business interruption section but no insurable interest for the purposes of the material damage section, meaning that there was no breach of the material damage proviso. The broader interest required by BI did not need to be insured by *Glengate* and the claim was paid.

This case confirms that the business interruption losses flowing from damage to uninsured property should be dealt with, assuming that the proviso has in the first instance been satisfied. The Glengate case did differentiate between a broad insurable interest and a more narrow personal interest. Whilst Glengate had a general insurable interest in the architect's drawings, it was not sufficiently narrow to require Glengate to have insured them. There was, therefore, no breach of the Material Damage Proviso.

## Waiver of The Material Damage Proviso

There are instances where insurers have waived the material damage proviso owing to the nature of the insured's business which may not involve generating revenue from physical assets.

**CHAPTER 2:**
# UNDERSTANDING THE ESSENTIALS OF COVER – PART 1

## 2.0 GENERAL INTRODUCTION

At the very core of business interruption insurance is the calculation of gross profit (or gross revenue) and the selection of the indemnity period. In between these two elements are several concepts which give clarity to the core cover. Such concepts include turnover, increase in cost of workings, wages, savings, etc. Experience has shown that these concepts are better understood when related to claims. We will attempt to x-ray these terms whilst keeping claims situations in mind. We will also play with the figures a bit. Claims will be dealt with in details in a subsequent chapter.

The Association of British Insurers (ABI) standard wording in respect of business interruption cover is as follows:

*"The insurance under Item No.1 (Gross Profit) is limited to Loss of Gross Profit due to a) Reduction in Turnover and b) Increase in Cost of Working and the amount payable as indemnity there under shall be:*

*a) in respect of Reduction in Turnover the sum produced by applying the Rate of Gross Profit to the amount by which the Turnover during the Indemnity Period shall fall short of the Standard Turnover in consequence of the Incident*

*b) in respect of Increase in Cost of Working, the additional expenditure (subject to the provisions of the Uninsured Standing Charges Clause) necessarily and reasonably incurred for the sole purpose of avoiding or diminishing the reduction in Turnover which but for that expenditure would have taken place during the Indemnity Period in consequence of the Incident, but not exceeding the sum produced by applying the Rate of Gross Profit to the amount of the reduction thereby avoided* less any sum saved during the indemnity period in respect of such of the charges and expenses of the Business payable out of Gross Profit as may cease or be reduced as a consequent of the Incident."

Standard definitions include the following:

"**Turnover**: The money paid or payable to the insured for goods sold and delivered and for services rendered in course of the Business at the Premises."

"**Indemnity Period**: The period beginning with the occurrence of the Incident and ending not later than the Maximum Indemnity Period thereafter during which the results of the Business shall be affected in consequence thereof."

"**Gross Profit**: The amount by which: i) the sum of the amount of the Turnover and the amounts of the closing stock and work in progress shall exceed ii) the sum of the amounts of the opening stock and work in progress and the amount of the Uninsured Working Expenses.

**Note**: The amount of the opening and closing stocks and work in progress shall be arrived at in accordance with the insured's normal accountancy methods, due provision being made for depreciation."

The policy provides for three elements of a business interruption loss computation. These comprise a **Loss of Gross Profit** (consequent upon a reduction in Turnover), **Increased Costs of Working** and **Savings**.

## Loss of Gross Profit

The impact of an incident upon a business is measured in terms of a decline in turnover. The turnover generated in those months in the previous year corresponding with the period affected by the insured incident is referred to as the Standard Turnover. For instance, if a fire occurred on 1$^{st}$ August 2018 and the business fully recovered from the effect on 1$^{st}$ December 2018, the turnover generated from 1st August 2017 to 1st December 2017 will be considered standard turnover. You may view this as a "control" turnover. This is then adjusted for any necessary trend such that it then represents the turnover that would have been anticipated but for the insured event. The company, for instance, may have acquired a new machine capable of producing at a faster pace in 2018 thus the standard turnover (2017 figures) will not be reflective of this hence the need for an adjustment. This is referred to as the Adjusted Standard Turnover. Actual turnover generated during the indemnity period (that is 1st August 2018 to 1st December 2018) is deducted from the Adjusted Standard Turnover to calculate the Reduction in Turnover.

Let us assume that the standard turnover is N1,000,000. As a result of business trend (the new machine or other factors), this has been adjusted to N1,200,000. If the actual turnover generated between 1st August 2018 to 1st December 2018 (indemnity period) is N500,000. The reduction in turnover will be N700,000 (1,200,000 – 500,000).

The Rate of Gross Profit (gross profit/annual turnover x 100) as defined in the policy is then applied to the Reduction in Turnover. If we assume that the rate of gross profit is 25%. The Loss of Gross Profit will be N175,000 (25% of 700,000). It is not necessary to compare levels of gross profit on a month by month basis pre and post-incident - the policy establishes the quantum of the loss initially on the turnover line. This avoids the complication that consideration and quantification of the greater number of variables that impact on gross profit would entail. The financial variation in the turnover can be more easily related directly back to the Damage.

The good news is, this item of cover relates to a Loss of Gross Profit consequent upon a Reduction in Turnover and not necessarily any Loss of Gross Profit from any other cause.

## Turnover

The definition of turnover relates to the operation of the business at the Premises. Were turnover to be derived to any significant degree off-site then clarification of this definition might be advisable. Businesses with long-term contracts may need to consider the term 'turnover' with some degree of care. An interim stage payment may have been received part way through a contract following which a catastrophic loss may be suffered which renders completion of the overall contract to be impractical. A return of the monies received to date may in certain circumstances be required. Such a repayment of funds would not constitute a loss of the turnover that would be reflected in the books but for the incident. The turnover, per accounting standards, may have been reflected in the accounts of a prior period. A loss which is a consequence of the incident, but not covered by the policy, might arise.

The policy wording implicitly assumes that physical damage will give rise to corresponding turnover losses within a defined period, such losses effectively commencing as at the date of the damage. Whilst this is generally a reasonable proposition, it need not be so. Earnings from royalties, for instance, would be unaffected by a fire incident and subsequent disruption in business. The consequences of Damage would result in royalties being depressed in the medium-term when the next generation of products should have been earning royalties but in reality, do not exist. A turnover loss would not arise within a twelve or even twenty-four-month Maximum Indemnity Period and potentially would never crystallise quickly enough for a claim to be submitted. That could be difficult to explain to the businessman who has paid a premium in respect of the business for many years.

In such a situation, it might be more meaningful to relate loss to the sales value of the loss of production time rather than requiring a turnover shortfall to crystallise.

Similarly, businesses generating income from annual subscriptions may not be in jeopardy until a future period. The future subscriptions for that period may not be secure if work to support them is not being done in the aftermath of an incident. Rather than provide a policy written on a standard gross profit basis, such businesses benefit more from policies written on the basis of a Loss of Output, translating the production loss into a financial loss on an agreed basis. Pre claim discussion as to how this should be calculated is always beneficial. Insurers can be satisfied that the basis on which premiums are received is consistent with the basis on which any future claim would be presented. Estimated Maximum Loss calculations can then be carried out with more certainty. The insured person benefits from knowing the basis on which a claim will be paid.

**Increased Cost of Working**

The policy allows for additional and reasonable costs incurred to prevent a Loss of Gross Profit arising, but not exceeding the amount that would be payable if the cost had not been incurred. This is known as the 'economic limit'. Overtime working by staff to avoid a loss of Turnover is a good example. In the way, hiring a new machine or factory to continue production would constitute an increase in the cost of working.

In the detailed wording, the increased cost cover is set out as item 1(b), the Gross Profit cover being item 1(a). On the policy schedule, it would be normal to show only the Gross Profit cover as item 1, but this does not mean that the increased cost cover is absent.

It is important to note that the economic limit is considered with reference to the profit at risk from the insurer's point of view. It is not restricted to the precise transaction that the costs are supporting. Notwithstanding the need to consider the economics of any cost incurred within the insured period, the insured business may wish to take a longer-term view, particularly in terms of key customers. A relatively modest customer this year may represent a significant account for the future and there is nothing to stop the insured business contributing to a cost themselves were it to be in their interest to do so to reflect the benefit of that expenditure to the business after the end of the Maximum Indemnity Period.

There is no requirement in the business interruption policy for an insured person to let either the insurer or the loss adjuster know if an increased cost is being incurred. It is either the cost is economically laid out to stop a loss accruing, which solely and directly derives from the insured incident, or it is not. This is also the position with Gross Losses, which would be claimable even if not formally quantified until the end of the indemnity period. That assumes the incident was nevertheless notified promptly and the loss properly mitigated.

In reality, it is greatly in the interest of the insured business to discuss all significant costs to be incurred in advance with the broker, insurers and/or loss adjusters. The latter will be liaising with the insured business in the event of a claim frequently and a mitigation strategy developed such that in the majority of cases the advisability of incurring any particular cost would have been discussed before the monies are spent.

In certain cases, the insured business may require the explicit support of the insurer before following a certain route. This reflects an increasingly proactive role undertaken by insurers in supporting businesses following major incidents. Watching from a distance and ultimately carrying out strict economic tests for costs and mitigation plans not previously discussed would be untenable. Of course, the insured person that does choose to keep the costs being incurred confidential will invite a strict retrospective economic appraisal. A transparent exchange of information between insurers/loss adjusters/brokers and the insured business facilitates interim payments post-loss, as well as allowing that business to benefit from the previous experience of disaster management that insurers have.

It is relevant to refer again to the fact that not all consequences of insured incidents are admissible items under a business interruption cover. There can be a perception that any additional cost not addressed under the material damage policy must by definition be an Increased Cost to be dealt with under the business interruption claim; that is not so. To be an admissible Increased Cost the policy definition must be met. If following a late delivery to a customer, a contractual liquidated payment is required, then that would not constitute an Increased Cost. It would derive primarily because of a historic contract and not in respect of a decision taken solely to avoid a future reduction in turnover. The fact that a future loss of turnover would no doubt accrue if the historic contractual requirement was not met would merely be incidental. It would not arise directly as a result of Damage. Such a cost can be insured under a Fines and Penalties extension. It is possible to expand the Increased Cost cover to remove the economic limit, (Additional Increase in Cost of Working cover).

**Savings**

The policy allows for the deduction of 'any sum saved' in respect of costs that would have been paid or payable but for the incident. These represent saved variable costs below the Gross Profit line that would have been incurred had there not been the operation of an insured peril. A simple example would be the fact that there will be a reduction in the variable electricity charge if a machine is not running.

The application of savings merely reflects the principle of indemnity. The only costs that would be deducted as variable costs represent those cash flows not deducted from turnover in defining gross profit that would not have occurred but for the incident but which in fact declined because of it. An insured person, in deducting costs from turnover to define gross profit, is assuming that such costs will decline in proportion to turnover, and asserting that such costs will be deducted from turnover in the event. The risk of the assumption lies with the insured business. The only costs deducted as savings are those that do actually reduce. The risk of assuming significant savings, therefore, lies with the underwriter in carrying out his Estimated Maximum Loss calculation.

**Wages/Payroll**

Recent trends have been to insure wages, payroll and salaries as part of the Gross Profit. This is often achieved by not listing wages as a specified working expense. This approach might have been influenced by the sophistication of the workforce, labour laws (e.g laws against casualisation of labour), labour unions, business continuity plans of companies, etc. It is important to note however that wages and payroll can be insured in several ways such as i) part of the gross profit ii) dual basis iii) dual payroll iv) 100% payroll.

The decision of the business as to how best to treat wages/payroll would usually be influenced by its very makeup. For instance, a company with a largely permanent and skilled workforce will opt to insure wages as part of the gross profit. Due to the factors highlighted above especially non-casualisation of labour, most organisations find themselves with permanent workers whether skilled or unskilled.

When it was possible to legally maintain a casual workforce, companies with significant wage expense in this category (casual and unskilled labour) often adopted the dual basis/dual payroll approach. This would require listing wages as part of the specified working expenses to delete it whilst expressly stating wages as an insured item with a specific sum insured. It could then be broken down into initial period, remainder period and option to consolidate. The final approach of 100% payroll meant wages and salaries would be insured as standing charges for the full maximum indemnity period.

## 2.1 THE WORKINGS OF THE BI POLICY

### 2.1.0 Gross Profit

The Gross Profit basis of cover is best used for manufacturing risks where a high element of the turnover comprises expenses that vary in direct proportion to it. An example is "purchases", which are already insured under the property policy or section as raw materials stock and could represent a good proportion of the turnover. If the Insured ceases to manufacture or has to reduce the output, the amount of purchases he will use will vary in direct proportion. By selecting items from the statement of financial position that will not be insured (uninsured variable costs or specified working expenses) it is possible to design the cover to reflect the Insured's likely Business Interruption exposure. Effectively we reduce the sum insured upon which the policy rate is based so that the Insured does not incur premium on items that he will not claim for under the Business Interruption policy.

One of the problems with Business Interruption Insurance is that terms such as Gross Profit and Gross Income used in insurance policies do not have the same meaning as they do in accounting. This usually creates misunderstanding between the accountants and the loss adjusters at the time of claim. Sadly, this is a common mistake which may not be realised until claim time, often with disastrous results for the policyholder. The difference in definition between Accounting Gross Profit and Insurable Gross Profit occurs most often in manufacturing risks.

**Accounting Gross Profit:** The cost accountant is trying to determine the exact cost of goods sold. All the costs of manufacture such as direct materials, direct labour and factory overheads are captured and deducted from sales turnover to arrive at Accounting Gross Profit.

**Insurable Gross Profit**: On the other hand, when it comes to Insurable Gross Profit under a Business Interruption Policy, it is only those expenses that vary in direct proportion to turnover or sales that ought to be deducted. Any fixed or semi-variable expense should be insured, whether it be above or below the Accounting Gross Profit line.

## What is Gross Profit?

Accountants Definition: Net Profit + Fixed Costs = Gross Profit. It must be noted that when a Trading Account is prepared, the accountant would usually arrive at the gross profit by deducting the cost of goods sold from the turnover. Cost of goods sold is opening stock plus purchases less closing stock. This method would naturally align with the insurer's definition. However, the challenge might lie with certain components such as factory wages.

**Policy Definition:** The amount by which: i) the sum of the amount of the Turnover and the amounts of the closing stock and work in progress shall exceed ii) the sum of the amounts of the opening stock and work in progress and the amount of the Uninsured Working Expenses (purchases, carriage, freight, etc.)

### 2.1.1: Gross Revenue

Gross Revenue basis is much simpler than Gross Profit. The Gross Revenue form insures the total turnover of the Business, without any deductions, for the length of the Maximum Indemnity Period. All we need to know is the annual turnover of the Business, which is something any Insured will know, and multiply it by the proportion which 12 months bears to the Maximum Indemnity Period. This model is best suited for the service industry given that the majority of their costs are staff and ICT related, so there is little to specify by way of variable costs. Office risks such as legal firms, audit firms, insurance brokers, insurance companies and so on would find the Gross

Revenue model most appropriate. What might need some further thought would be the likely Indemnity Periods required, as some businesses may recover quicker than others. The telecommunication and ICT industry is a good example.

### 2.1.2: Gross Profit or Gross Revenue, What should it be?

There is often a significant level of underinsurance when it comes to the sum insured for Gross Profit. One of the factors contributing to this level of underinsurance is thought to be the lack of clarity associated with the Gross Profit wording. Many policyholders do not fully appreciate that Gross Profit as defined in an insurance policy is often calculated differently than it is in the commercial/accounting world. This leads to under-declaration and of course underinsurance. As a result, insurers do not receive the correct premium for the risk and the policyholder does not receive a full indemnity when a loss occurs.

Most often, when the level of cover or sum insured is discussed at a renewal meeting with the broker, the policyholder can offer a reliable figure for turnover or gross revenue with a high degree of certainty. However, if the rate of Gross Profit used by the business is different from the rate that should be applied under the policy wording, both the policyholder and the broker will likely underestimate the sum insured. As a result, the level of premium charged for the risk will be too low and in the event of a claim, the policyholder will find that their loss will be reduced through the operation of average. Often, this leads to the dissatisfied policyholder who may sue its broker for professional negligence.

Experts the world over are beginning to propose that how the sum insured is calculated (and the risk is rated) should be altered from Gross Profit to Gross Revenue. This change seems to offer significant benefits to policyholders, brokers and insurers. While a proportion of policyholders may elect to deliberately underinsure, the majority do so unknowingly. This is usually because the policyholder misunderstands how the Gross Profit sum insured should be calculated. Gross Profit is usually calculated differently by a business than is required by an insurance policy. A good example is the treatment of wages; in business, Gross Profit is calculated net of wages, whereas wages are usually included in the definition of Gross Profit in most insurance policies. This is particularly the case with manufacturers but certainly not exclusively so.

If Gross Revenue were insured, this confusion would not arise and the risk of a policyholder underinsuring would be reduced. In addition to reducing the risk of underinsurance, several other practical situations may benefit from the change. Replacing Gross Profit as the standard basis of rating with Gross Revenue will be a significant and fundamental alteration and will not be without its challenges.

The following is a summary of some key points that may need to be considered:

i. the basis of rating will need to be changed to reflect the adoption of much higher sums insured;
ii. the reinsurance arrangements will, in many cases, need to be reassessed and reset;
iii. policy extensions, for example, a supplier's extension will need to be altered to a Gross Revenue basis.
iv. The wording concerning the Increase in Cost of Working (ICW) cover would need to be modified. For example, ICW would take its economic test at the Gross Revenue level.
v. There is a risk that insurers' exposure to Increase

in Cost of Working (ICW) and the likely payments made in connection with ICW may increase. However, such ICW would still need to satisfy a 'necessary, fair and reasonable' test. Besides, the introduction of a higher threshold for the economic test would mean that payments under any 'Additional Increased Costs of Working' (AICW) extension would be far less frequent.

**CHAPTER 3:**
# UNDERSTANDING THE ESSENTIALS OF COVER – PART 2

## 3.1.0: MAXIMUM INDEMNITY PERIOD

The Maximum Indemnity Period is generally defined as *'the period beginning with the occurrence of the Incident and ending not later than the Maximum Indemnity Period thereafter during which the results of the Business shall be affected in consequence thereof'*. If we have a maximum indemnity period of say 12 months, it would mean that if an incident occurred on 1st January 2019 and the impact on the business lasted till 1st March 2020, our maximum indemnity period will be 1st January 2019 to 31st December 2019 being 12 months. The impact from 1st January 2020 to 1st March 2020 would have occurred outside the maximum indemnity period thus not covered by the policy.

As previously mentioned, an Incident is usually defined as *'Loss or destruction of or damage to property used by the Insured at the Premises for the purpose of the Business'*. The results of the business include sales/gross profit, increased costs and savings. In addition, under the alternative trading clause, the impact of goods sold elsewhere also needs to be specifically accounted for during the Maximum Indemnity Period.

By responding to the period during which the results of the business are affected, a policy in the UK and most policies in Nigeria provides cover during the period of repair and subsequently while the business rebuilds its customer base, ending no later than the expiry of the Maximum Indemnity Period. The application is different from US policy form, which usually provides cover only during the period of repair, sometimes with a short, additional 'build-up' allowance.

Policyholders may assume that the Indemnity Period relates to the period during which results are depressed rather than affected. Sometimes, and while this is not normally the case, assets reinstated after an incident can generate more business than would have been the case had an incident not occurred. This could be as a result of improvements in the building or equipment.

The business might feel the results are back to normal once turnover reaches the level it would have been but for the damage. They may be surprised if the adjuster seeks to argue at that stage that some of the sales revenue lost in the earlier part of the Indemnity Period is subsequently clawed back. This surprise may be worsened by the fact that the policy makes specific provision for alternative trading but is not explicit on the clawback issue (i.e., where an initial loss is less than a benefit subsequently experienced).

The issue can be complicated if the insured has at its own expense upgraded its production facility which itself results in extra capacity and revenue. As the above problems relate to the 'build-up' period after the repairs are complete, they tend not to arise under a US policy form. As a way out of this challenge, policies could clarify the definition of the Indemnity Period to include words such as 'during which the results of the Business shall be **adversely or positively** affected'.

The key task for the insured is determining the appropriate maximum indemnity period. The length of the Indemnity Period is important from two perspectives. All cover ceases on the expiry of the Indemnity Period so if it is set too short and does not allow for a full recovery of the Business then the Insured may not receive an adequate indemnity. Secondly, the premium is based upon the related multiple of the annual Gross Profit or Gross Revenue, so the longer the Indemnity Period the more premium will be required.

This inevitably produces something of a dilemma for the insured or anyone advising an insured. If the insured is given a technically incorrect (too short) Indemnity Period, then he may sue his adviser when a policy fails to provide a proper indemnity. If the premium is made artificially high, by setting a strictly technically correct, but perhaps realistically overly long Indemnity Period, then the business may be lost to a competitor on price if the competition takes a more robust view of the potential recovery of the business.

It is generally preferable to provide a variety of options for any insured to consider, which then puts the onus back on the insured to properly consider their risk and their likely recovery potential. Generally, a manufacturing company is likely to require a longer Indemnity Period to regain their anticipated prior loss trading level than a service firm. However, whether the cover is Gross Profit or Gross Revenue, similar criteria apply. For larger concerns, it would be normal to consider each site as a separate risk and evaluate the individual exposure, and then to consider mitigating factors such as spare capacity in other parts of the group that could assist reduce that exposure.

**Criteria for Selecting the Maximum Indemnity Period**

When thinking about the Indemnity Period length, we need to consider the worst case scenario and work back from that. The following criteria would guide:

a) Thinking/decision time: When an incident occurs, decisions have to be made. These may be simply applying the business continuity plan (BCP). With a major loss, however, there might be opportunities. The business might consider relocating or significantly upgrading its facilities rather than just reinstating.

The high-level management thinking and planning will all take time, often many, many months to resolve and all the while the clock is ticking.

b) Planning consents and enquiries: It is common knowledge that obtaining building/planning permits/consents can take a very long time. The government can even refuse permission to reinstate as their overall planning has changed the use of the area from commercial to residential housing for instance. This, in turn, will bring about fresh planning needs to move elsewhere.

c) Re-building/building time: Interestingly, this portion of exposure is probably the easiest to determine and can often be much shorter than imagined for a new build. If the Insured has a clear hand, reinstating on a new site with modern materials is often a very quick option indeed. Reinstatement on-site, however, can be fraught with difficulties, ranging from lengthy debris removal/pollution clean up time to sourcing correct materials for listed building reinstatement.

d) Lead time for replacement machinery/plant: In manufacturing entities, many machines are bespoke and can take anything up to a year to replace. In Nigeria, the issue of port congestion can sometimes add to the lead time. This would not be the case in most service industries where the majority of equipment is available off the shelf within days or weeks. However, switching stations and hubs for telecoms companies, for example, would take much longer to replace so it is vital to understand the make-up of the business and where the bottlenecks are, along with any mitigating factors such as spare capacity/redundancy elsewhere.

e) Re-training staff: It is inevitable that in a long interruption staff would have been laid off so it is important to build in time to train new staff and to re-train existing staff in any new processes introduced in reinstating the business.

f) Re-commissioning plant/systems: We need to consider both partial loss situations as well as a total replacement. Most often, attempting to integrate new replacement kit/equipment with pre-existing undamaged items often causes more trouble than starting up a whole new plant or system.

g) Regaining anticipated pre-loss trading level: "Extra" time to regain market position is a key component of the UK BI form which is also applicable in Nigeria, as long as the Indemnity Period is set long enough. It must be noted that pure "loss of market" is not covered.

### Indemnity Period Vs Maximum Indemnity Period

The policy is not meant to provide unlimited coverage in terms of period otherwise business interruption losses will go on for years. There has to be a cut-off point which will allow realistic estimates of amounts and premiums. The policyholder can choose for how long after the Damage has happened they would want to be able to claim business interruption losses. This period is the Maximum Indemnity Period (MIP).

The Indemnity Period usually starts at the date of Damage and ends when the business is no longer affected by it, or at the end of the maximum indemnity period. The actual period affected is known as the Indemnity Period and the Maximum Indemnity Period is the point at
which the policy ceases to respond.

### 3.2.0: UNDERSTANDING VARIABLE COST AND THE GROSS PROFIT MODEL

As mentioned previously, there is a difference between the accountant's view of gross profit and that of the insurer. It all comes down to which variable cost will be insured or not.

The Gross Profit basis of cover is best used for manufacturing risks where a high element of the turnover comprises expenses that vary in direct proportion to it. An example is "purchases", which are already insured under the property policy or section as raw material stock and could represent a significant amount of the turnover. If the Insured ceases to manufacture or has to reduce the output, the amount of purchases they will use will vary in direct proportion.

By selecting items that will not be insured (uninsured variable costs or specified working expenses) we can design the cover to reflect the Insured's likely BI exposure. Effectively we reduce the sum insured upon which the policy rate is based so that the Insured does not incur premium on items that they will not claim for under the BI policy.

If we examine a typical statement of comprehensive income (profit or loss account), the following headings will come up. We would, however, check if these are variable costs or not.

**Rental income:** This could swing either way depending on the source. Where does this income come from? Is it from letting premises on the same site or elsewhere? If it is on the same site then it needs to be included in the exposed turnover (i.e. not excluded) as the Insured will lose income from it if the factory burns down.

**Opening stock and work in progress:** This is the valuation of the residual stock and works in progress at the factory at the beginning of the financial year. It forms part of the formula for defining the policy Gross Profit. The item does not need mentioning in the list of variable cost

**Closing stock and work in progress:** This is the (estimated) valuation of what will be left unused or unsold in the factory at the close of the financial year. Again it forms part of the formula and will when the figures are validated, give us a differential between what the factory started and finished the year with. The item does not need mentioning in the list of variable cost

**Purchases:** As mentioned above, purchases often form a major part of a manufacturing company's turnover and will usually vary in direct proportion to turnover earned. This item should be on the list of uninsured variable costs.

**Factory wages:** These will, of course, vary, but not necessarily in direct proportion. There are too many unknown quantities to be prescriptive. During a long interruption, most shop
floor staff will be laid off and only taken back when the factory is ready to resume production. On the other hand, during a short interruption, it may be prudent to spend more money than usual on wages as overtime payments to maintain production. It follows that no solution fits all circumstances and so it is normal to include them in full but to expect the rate to be discounted to reflect any anticipated reduced exposure, so equity is achieved. The item should *not* be on the list but does appear on the accountant's list of deductions in arriving at Gross Profit.

**Outworkers/Outsource staff:** Manufacturers, particularly small ones, often use outsource staff to do jobs that are either specialised or difficult to do in a factory environment. If the factory burns down, they will still be carrying on their job, unless their stocks are held totally at the factory. The components could, in any event, be supplied direct and they would then build up a stockpile for future use when the factory gets back in operation. On the face of it would seem sensible *not* to exclude them from the turnover, particularly as the amount is hardly going to make much difference to the premium.

**Subcontractors:** Subcontractors frequently feature in the manufacturing chain. Assuming a total loss at the factory, there would be no inputs unless there was a stock of them held off-site, it would appear that payments to these subcontractors are likely to cease, so they should appear on the list of uninsured variable cost.

**Packing and freight:** Both these items are to do with outwards goods, so if nothing is being made they will cease, assuming there is no agreement with the carrier to the contrary. With this caveat in mind, they should appear on the list.

**Discounts on purchases:** Discounts will vary in direct proportion to the level of purchases so need to be on the list, but in a negative sense. They need to be deducted from the purchases figure, as they will reduce as the purchases fall.

**Salaries:** In much the same way as we do not exclude wages, we also do not exclude salaries.
Generally, most salaried staff are kept on following a loss and will be needed to actively plan and implement the recovery.

**Salesman's commissions:** This is an interesting one to debate. Certainly, if there is nothing to sell then there can be no commission. However, if the insured want to retain high performing sales staff they are unlikely to do so on basic salary terms, or minimum commissions may be included in the salesman's contract. For a total loss situation, it would be safer to leave the figure, or at least a proportion of it, in the Gross Profit calculation so that the business can get back on its feet quickly by using good quality salesmen to sell goods before re-opening for later delivery.

**Power, light and heat:** Again, we would need to ask some questions. What do the insured mean by "power?" Is it high amperage electrical supply (external supply), or is it gas/diesel (generated internally) for running the factory or both? Once that is established we also need to know if they have any unbreakable agreements with the supply authorities. Whatever the answers may be, we need to be careful not to stifle the recovery of the business by cutting off its power, light and heat! We could perhaps consider excluding a percentage of the cost in the event of a total loss.

**Advertising:** This is another debatable item. On the face of it, all advertising will cease once there is nothing to sell. However, the Insured may well wish to spend more than the allotted budget advertising a return to business so it would be sensible to either keep the item in or only exclude a portion of it.

**Postage/telephone/stationery/sundries:** These office-related expenses are likely to continue. They should not be on the list.

**Rent and rates/insurance/bank charges:** Rent may fall depending on what the rent clause says, but rates will continue, as will insurance and bank charges. Indeed, one could expect the insurance premium to go up to enable the insurer to recoup some of the loss.

**Maintenance:** This will vary, although not necessarily in direct proportion. It should be on the list, at least for further discussion.

**Depreciation:** Again, this will vary and should be on the list for further discussion. Some brokers feel this should be deleted altogether as it is largely a "fictitious" accounting device to write off assets and can be challenged as a saving by adjusters. However, if we do that there will be nothing in the pot for a partial loss or off-site loss when on-site assets may still depreciate, and maybe faster than before if any undamaged ones are made to work harder.

**Bad debts:** These are often taken as a fixed proportion of turnover, so should be on the list.

### 3.3.0: DEALING WITH INFLATION

When considering an adequate sum insured or policy limit to counter inflation we need to take into account the anticipated turnover for the policy period, and project it forward to be adequate for an incident occurring on the last day of the policy and also sufficient to cover inflation up to the expiry of the Maximum Indemnity Period. If the amount so declared is inadequate average will apply to the loss.

**Declaration linked basis.**
A method has evolved which generally deals with this problem called "Declaration
Linked." The insured declares the estimated Gross Profit or Revenue for the
Indemnity Period at inception or renewal. Insurers allow a maximum of 33.3% uplift
in the estimated sum insured and waive the application of average. However, this may not be so generous as it appears, as built into the wording is an adjustment feature whereby the Insured has to declare the actual Gross Profit or Gross Revenue earned at the end of each policy period and the premium is adjusted either upwards or downwards accordingly.

Downward adjustments are capped at 50% of the deposit premium charged, whereas upwards adjustments are unlimited, irrespective of the 33.3% cap placed on the uplift.
Nevertheless, this system has stood the test of time and is generally recognised as being beneficial to most medium/large scale insureds.

There are three main difficulties encountered with this concept:

**1. Rapidly growing businesses:** New (startup) businesses often expand at a far greater rate than the 33.3% factor allowed. It is difficult to achieve an equitable rate for higher rates of inflation, so it is often necessary to deal with these on a conventional basis. It is sensible to review the likely maximum sum insured required every quarter, until the expansion
has settled down to a level sustainable within the usual 33.3% margin for inflation.

**2. Declining businesses:** This will be a fairly rare occurrence as the purchase of BI may be questionable anyway. However, if a business is in decline rather than expansion, there is no need for the inflation factor and there may be insufficient return premium available should

the decline be beyond 50%. In these rather extreme circumstances, it would be appropriate to review the cover required regularly, cutting off cover entirely when it becomes obvious that an Insured incident will no longer affect earnings, as there will be no business to support.

**3. Covers placed on a first loss basis:** If a first loss basis is used the inflation factor may be meaningless in a total loss situation for a policy covering a single location as the policy limit will be the maximum amount claimable, irrespective of inflation. However, for multiple location risks, Insurers will continue to apply the 33.3% uplift to individual declarations so there is value in maintaining the declaration linked basis, as long as the phrases used reflect

the terms "limit" rather than "sum insured" as so often happens.

### 3.4.0 COMPUTING GROSS PROFIT SUM INSURED – WORKED EXAMPLE

The following figures were supplied by the ED Finance of Afang Plc.

| | | |
|---|---|---|
| Turnover | 3,000,000.00 | |
| Purchases | 1,500,000.00 | |
| Opening Stock 01/01/2017 | | 440,000.00 |
| Opening WIP as @ 01/01/17 | | 190,000.00 |
| Closing Stock as @ 31/12/17 | | 290,000.00 |
| Closing WIP as @ 31/12/2017 | | 135,000.00 |
| Direct Wages | 127,000.00 | |
| Packaging Materials | | 288,000.00 |

Carriage              75,000.00

Power         25,000.00

Rent and Rates        75,000.00

Depreciation          150,000.00

Lightening and Heating        80,000.00

Advertising           60,000.00

You are expected to assist the company to calculate the sum insured for Gross Profit (2018 and 2019) bearing in mind that this policy is written on a difference basis and is based on a 12 month maximum indemnity period. This business is expected to grow by 10% in 2018 and 15% in 2019. Inflation rate could be in the region of 5% annually.

**Suggested Solution to Worked Example**

Using the difference basis, the gross profit will be computed as follows:

| | | |
|---|---|---|
| Turnover | 3,000,000.00 | |
| Closing stock as @ 31\12\17 | | 290,000.00 |
| Closing WIP as @ 31\12\17 | | <u>135,000.00</u> |
| | | **3,425,000.00** |
| Less | | |
| Opening stock as @ 01\01\17 | | 440,000.00 |
| Opening WIP as @ 01\01\17 | | 190,000.00 |
| Purchases | 1,500,000.00 | |
| Packaging materials | 288,000.00 | |
| Carriage | <u>75,000.00</u> | |
| | | <u>**2,493,000.00**</u> |
| Gross profit | **932,000.00** | |

Given the projected growth, an allowance should be made for the effect of growth for the business for 10% in 2018 and 15% in 2019. Also, the inflation rate which would be in the region of 5% must be considered.

2018 Projected Gross Profit Sum Insured with Inflation will be thus:

= (Gross Profit + growth rate) + inflation rate

= (932,000 + 10%) + 5%

= 932,000 + 93,200 + 51,260

= 1,076,460.00

2019 Projected Gross Profit Sum Insured with Inflation will be thus:

= 2018 Projected Gross Profit + growth rate + inflation rate

= (1,076,460 + 15%) + 5%

= 1,076,460 + 161,469 + 61,896

= 1,299,825.00

# CHAPTER 4:
# RATING THE POLICY

## 4.1 INTRODUCTION

It must be mentioned that in Nigeria, the BI policy is still being rated based on tariff as stated in the Nigeria Insurers Association's Fire Rating Guide of 1999. This document has not been revised in over two decades and has grossly failed to accommodate new risks areas. Other countries of the world most notably the UK jettisoned tariff rating as far back as 1985. Insurers are therefore expected to rate the policy based on their models.

Based on the Fire Rating Guide issued by NIA (Nigeria Insurers Association), the basis rate is that of the Fire/Material Damage as stipulated by NIA. The recommended basis rate multipliers for gross profit and auditors fees are stated below.

1. **GROSS PROFIT**

Recommended Basis Rate Multipliers

| INDEMNITY PERIOD RATE | PERCENTAGES OF THE BASIS |
|---|---|
| Not exceeding 3 months | 75% |
| "       "       4   " | 90% |
| "       "       6   " | 110% |
| "       "       9   " | 130% |
| "       "       12  " | 150% |
| "       "       15  " | 145% |
| "       "       18  " | 140% |
| "       "       24  " | 125% |
| "       "       30  " | 120% |
| "       "       36  " | 115% |
| "       "       48  " | 110% |
| "       "       60  " | 105% |
| "       "       72  " | 100% |

Exceeding 72 " 95%

## 2. AUDITORS FEES

125% of Basis Rate

## 3. WAGES

**WAGES**

Dual Basis Wages Mutiplier

As stated in the table overleaf

(a) The Mutiplier show are minimum to be applied for the indeminity Period selected and should be increase for any adverse features.

(b) Existing policies to be amended at renewal.

**CONSEQUENTIAL LOSS INSURANCE**
**TABLE OF DUAL BASIS WAAGES**

| INDEMNITY PERIOD | INITIAL PERIOD OF 100% COVER | PERCENTAGE OF WAGES INSURED FOR THE REMAINDER OF THE INDEMINTY PERIOD |||||||||||||||||
|---|---|---|---|---|---|---|---|---|---|---|---|---|---|---|---|---|---|
| | | 10% || 15 || 20 || 25 || 33 1/3 || 40 || 50 || 66 2/3 || 75 ||
| | | A | B | A | B | A | B | A | B | A | B | A | B | A | B | A | B | A | B |
| 12 MONTHS | 4 | 55% | 7 | 59% | 9 | 64% | 10 | 66% | 10 | 76% | 13 | 83% | 16 | 94% | 19 | 113% | 20 | 112% | 33 |
| | 5 | 60% | 9 | 64% | 10 | 67% | 10 | 72% | 12 | 80% | 15 | 87% | 16 | 98% | 22 | 115% | 29 | 124% | 36 |
| | 6 | 63% | 10 | 66% | 10 | 70% | 12 | 75% | 13 | 83% | 16 | 90% | 17 | 100% | 22 | 117% | 29 | 125% | 36 |
| | 8 | 69% | 10 | 71% | 12 | 76% | 13 | 81% | 15 | 88% | 17 | 99% | 19 | 104% | 24 | 119% | 33 | 127% | 36 |
| | 13 | 83% | 16 | 86% | 16 | 90% | 17 | 94% | 19 | 100% | 22 | 105% | 24 | 113% | 29 | 125% | 36 | 131% | 39 |
| | 26 | 114% | 29 | 116% | 29 | 118% | 33 | 120% | 33 | 123% | 36 | 126% | 36 | 130% | 39 | 137% | 42 | 140% | 46 |
| 18 MONTHS | 4 | 41% | 9 | 46% | 12 | 49% | 13 | 54% | 15 | 64% | 19 | 71% | 24 | 83% | 36 | 102% | 54 | 11% | 58 |
| | 5 | 45% | 12 | 49% | 13 | 52% | 15 | 58% | 16 | 67% | 22 | 74% | 26 | 85% | 39 | 103% | 54 | 11% | 61 |
| | 6 | 46% | 12 | 50% | 16 | 59% | 16 | 60% | 17 | 69% | 24 | 76% | 29 | 87% | 39 | 104% | 54 | 11% | 61 |
| | 8 | 49% | 13 | 54% | 15 | 59% | 17 | 64% | 19 | 72% | 26 | 79% | 33 | 89% | 42 | 106% | 56 | 118% | 62 |
| | 13 | 59% | 17 | 64% | 19 | 68% | 22 | 73% | 26 | 80% | 33 | 88% | 39 | 95% | 49 | 110% | 58 | 123% | 67 |
| | 26 | 80% | 33 | 83% | 36 | 87% | 39 | 90% | 42 | 96% | 49 | 100% | 52 | 107% | 56 | 118% | 63 | 122% | 67 |
| 24 MONTHS | 4 | 59% | 7 | 59% | 9 | 64% | 10 | 66% | 10 | 76% | 13 | 83% | 16 | 94% | 19 | 113% | 20 | 122% | 72 |
| | 5 | 36% | 12 | 38% | 13 | 43% | 16 | 48% | 19 | 57% | 29 | 64% | 39 | 74% | 52 | 91% | 65 | 100% | 77 |
| | 6 | 37% | 13 | 40% | 15 | 45% | 17 | 50% | 22 | 58% | 29 | 65% | 39 | 75% | 52 | 92% | 67 | 100% | 77 |
| | 8 | 38% | 13 | 43% | 16 | 48% | 19 | 53% | 24 | 61% | 33 | 67% | 42 | 77% | 54 | 92% | 67 | 101% | 79 |
| | 13 | 40% | 17 | 51% | 22 | 55% | 26 | 59% | 33 | 67% | 42 | 72% | 49 | 81% | 56 | 93% | 67 | 103% | 79 |
| 30 MONTHS | 26 | 62% | 36 | 66% | 39 | 69% | 40 | 73% | 49 | 78% | 54 | 83% | 58 | 90% | 65 | 102% | 76 | 108% | 81 |
| | 39 | 71% | 46 | 74% | 52 | 77% | 54 | 80% | 56 | 85% | 60 | 89% | 65 | 95% | 69 | 106% | 78 | 110% | 82 |
| | 52 | 80% | 56 | 83% | 58 | 85% | 60 | 88% | 60 | 92% | 67 | 95% | 69 | 100% | 74 | 108% | 81 | 113% | 87 |
| 36 MONTHS | 4 | 23% | 12 | 28% | 16 | 33% | 22 | 38% | 29 | 47% | 46 | 54% | 56 | 64% | 69 | 81% | 100 | 89% | 112 |
| | 5 | 25% | 13 | 30% | 17 | 35% | 24 | 40 | 33 | 48% | 49 | 59% | 58 | 65% | 71 | 82% | 100 | 90% | 115 |
| | 6 | 27% | 15 | 31% | 19 | 36% | 26 | 41% | 36 | 49% | 49 | 58% | 60 | 66% | 74 | 82% | 100 | 90% | 115 |
| | 8 | 29% | 16 | 34% | 22 | 38% | 29 | 43% | 39 | 51% | 54 | 58% | 63 | 67% | 74 | 83% | 104 | 91% | 112 |
| | 13 | 34% | 22 | 38% | 29 | 43% | 39 | 48% | 49 | 55% | 58 | 61% | 67 | 70% | 78 | 85% | 107 | 93% | 120 |
| | 26 | 45% | 42 | 48% | 49 | 52% | 54 | 58% | 60 | 63% | 69 | 68% | 76 | 76% | 89 | 89% | 112 | 95% | 122 |
| | 39 | 51% | 54 | 54% | 56 | 58% | 63 | 61% | 67 | 67% | 74 | 72% | 81 | 79% | 92 | 91% | 117 | 97% | 125 |
| | 52 | 57% | 60 | 60% | 65 | 63% | 69 | 68% | 74 | 72% | 81 | 76% | 89 | 83% | 104 | 93% | 120 | 99% | 128 |

Percentage of basis rate applied to Annual Wage Roll Mutiple therefore if indemnity Period exceeds 12 months
The Number of weeks of alternative Insurance

## 4.2.0 RATING CONSIDERATIONS

Despite the above reality in Nigeria, there are basic underwriting considerations and risk criteria that must be considered when rating a business interruption policy. The book aims to deal with standard rating practice and not the tariff basis used in Nigeria. With tariff rating, it is simply a matter of multiplying the rates on the sum insured. Key underwriting considerations are often lost in the process.

When rating a business interruption policy, two main underwriting considerations are (a) Factors which cannot easily be changed for the better e.g the business of the proposer, premises, trade process, heating system, other occupants. (b) Factors which can be changed for the better e.g waste control, congestion control, workflow, maintenance, cleanliness, training, portable heaters, segregation, fire extinguishment.

Usually, a proper risks survey would have identified the above factors which would guide the underwriter in assessing the risks. The following items would generally constitute risks criteria: Trade, Acceptance Category, Moral Hazard, Physical Hazard, Risks/insured indices, Size of Insurance, etc. Ultimately, the insurer would be looking at the basic premium, expected losses, commission, margin of profit and other management expenses in determining the premium. This will not ignore other factors such as competition, inflation and other rates.

### 4.2.1: RATING OF GROSS PROFIT AND GROSS REVENUE POLICIES

The traditional starting point is the average contents rate for material damage. This is because the insured may or may not own the buildings in which they operate, but they are almost certainly going to own and control the contents which will have the most bearing on the likely inception hazard of losses. Fire and "dry" perils (lightning, explosion, aircraft, earthquake, riot, malicious damage) will have the most impact on the business and the rates for these are taken in full. Wet perils (storm, flood, burst pipes and impact and the accidental damage element of "all risks) are not so likely to result in a severe interruption to the Business so a reduced rate is usually applied for consequential loss. Hence the makeup of a business interruption rate for Gross Profits or Revenue would consist of the following:

The fire rate less any fire extinguishing appliances discounts as given for in the material damage cover. Besides insurers traditionally allow a further discount for sprinklers as this method of protection has been proven to dramatically reduce the impact of consequential loss from fire in the range 33.3% to 50%.

Plus: dry perils: the full material damage rate
Plus: wet perils: usually 50% of the material damage rate.

An underwriter would then look at the interruption features of the particular risk to see if any positive features make it attractive and could justify further discounts, such as:

**Spread of premises**
If the client occupies several premises such as a supermarket chain or a bank, the likelihood of a severe loss is diminished by the sheer number of premises, only one or two of which could be affected by an incident at any one time.

**Internal assistance**
Perhaps not all locations are working at full capacity so in the event of an interruption it might be possible to move production elsewhere to mitigate the loss.

**Duplication of process**
Similar to the above, but more usually on the same site, where in the event of a partial loss, the Insured could invoke overtime arrangements and makeup production from a duplicate line.

**Buffer stocks**
If the insured hold several months supply of buffer stocks of finished goods which are
unaffected by the incident, they could draw these off and use

them to bolster sales to
mitigate the loss during the interruption. However, modern business practice makes this less likely as accountants regard buffer stocks as wasted assets, and will do their best to make sure they are maintained at minimum levels, if at all.

## Adjustment for the Indemnity Period

Under a tariff rating regime, this adjustment is not necessary as the fire rating and multiplier would have taken care of this. In a non-tariff structure, the rate arrived at is then adjusted for the length of the Indemnity Period and applied to the sum insured, which is the appropriate multiple of the annual budget figure. The longer the Indemnity Period the less chance of a total interruption and hence the multiplier rate is reduced similar to those of NIA stated above.

An Indemnity Period of fewer than 12 months is not normally viable as insurers invariably use the full 12 months figure and apply a small discount to the rate, so usually, it is more economic to stick with a minimum of 12 months Indemnity Period on conventional policies. Please note that this might not be the same for ICT, Telecommunication, Payment System Providers and similar organisations whose nature of business requires a very short indemnity period.

## Deductibles

For larger risks, a combined deductible is often requested which will apply to both the
material damage and business interruption loss. In practice, any combined deductible
such as this is likely to be absorbed by the material damage settlement so underwriters rarely consider it justifiable to further discount the business interruption premium for combined deductibles. A separate time deductible is much more attractive and is often the preferred method when an underwriter needs to impose a deductible to eliminate minor losses. Again time de-

ductible may not be useful for businesses who cannot afford even a 24 hours interruption due to the nature of their operations.

## 4.2.2 RATING OF INCREASE IN COST OF WORKING (ICOW) - BUSINESSES OPERATING ENTIRELY AS OFFICES (INCREASE OFFICE EXPENSES)

This is a more restricted form of cover and may be chosen by some businesses, whose income would not be reduced in the event of physical damage to the insured's property. Typically these are office-type risks who only need a temporary office from which to conduct their business. These will be the businesses of professional people whose activities are restricted to the selling of a service such as building societies, banks, insurance companies, insurance brokers, legal firms and so on. There was a case of an insurance broking firm whose head office annex collapsed at Maryland, Lagos in 2010. The company was able to continue operations in a matter of hours and claim lodged with the insurance company for increased cost of working succeeded. For Increased Costs, only the rates will often be pre-set by the Insurer concerned and will not necessarily appear to be linked to the particular material damage risk features, although rates will be modified according to the Maximum Indemnity Period.

Unlike full value covers, discounts for sprinklered risks are not normally given and set coverage is given for the full range of perils so often no reductions are available for a limited selection. As the insurer could suffer a loss at any time at any one of the premises the rate is applied to the Limit of Liability multiplied by the number of premises covered. Ordinarily, the base rate will be calculated in accordance with the methods described above for Gross Profit or Gross Revenue, etc) multiplied by the ICOW rating factor.

### ICOW rating factor
Where restricted settlement provisions apply (for example, the maximum payable in the first three months of the MIP is 25%)

and there is a division of amount between separate buildings the Rating Factor might be 3.0 i.e. if the base rate arrived at on a standard Gross Profit basis is 0.15%; the rate for ICOW only is 0.15% x 3.0 = 0.45% applied to the limit of loss. As stated above the resultant premium should apply per premises.

### 4.2.3 RATING OF ADDITIONAL INCREASE IN COST OF WORKING (AICOW)

This is a separate item available as an addition to the main earnings item (e.g. Gross Profit, etc) covering recoverable costs that exceed the economic limit. The same rate, inclusive of discounts and loadings that are applied to the main item are also applied to the AICOW limit without any further adjustment. At first glance, this appears to be in contradiction to the rating shown above imposed on ICOW items only but it reflects the view that the item may not be called upon to pay as most increased costs will fall within Item 1b of the policy, which has already been taken into account in the policy rating.

### 4.2.4 RATING OF FLEXIBLE LIMIT OF LOSS COVERS

Initially, the same procedure as described in rating full value (e.g. Gross Profit, etc) covers is followed to produce a full value premium when applied to the sum insured. The premium is then discounted for the first loss element dependant upon the percentage of the loss limit in relation to the EML / PML (estimated maximum loss/probable maximum loss).

For example, Total 12 months Sum Insured 250M
EML/PML is 75M
Limit of Loss is 10M
Limit of Loss as a percentage to the EML / PML is 13.33% (10m/75m x 100)

The discount to be given from the full value premium in the above case may be in the range of 40/50%. The closer the first loss limit gets to the PML, the less the discount, although underwriters rarely give away more than 50% of the premium required for the full value risk.

**CHAPTER 5:**
# POLICY DESIGN AND EXTENSIONS –PART 1

We did mention in chapter 1 how the definitions of *The Insured*, *The Business* and *The Premises* are all key to triggering a business interruption claim. When designing a business interruption programme we need to particularly investigate the business and any premises used, as unless they are correctly specified the policy may not respond in the event of a claim. Often we need to *extend* the definitions to provide the full cover that the Insured requires. In this chapter, we will demonstrate how clauses can be used to extend and clarify the cover provided.

## 5.1 EXPANDING THE CORE COVER

The core business interruption cover relates to Damage from an insured peril to property used for the purpose of the business at the Premises. In many cases, it might be desirable to arrange for cover from insured events at other locations, such as those of customers or suppliers. Ultimately, these extensions expand the concept of Premises. In other instances, additional perils can be insured against at the Premises already identified, expanding the scope of the existing cover. Engineering breakdown is an example.

Some extensions do not fit either of the above categories, not being related to fixed locations, nor introducing new perils at the Premises themselves. Denial of Access and Loss of Attraction cover are examples of this, dealing with events that might occur in the locality of the Premises, although still requiring Damage in the vicinity. The most common extensions have been considered below.

### 5.1.1 ADDITIONAL INCREASE IN COST OF WORKING

The core business interruption cover provides for increased costs to be incurred to avoid a loss of Gross Profit, but not exceeding the amount of the profit loss thereby avoided (the economic limit). It is possible to extend the insurance such that any amount of money can be spent as long as it is reasonable and necessary for the business, without reference to any such economic limit, and this is what the Additional Increase in Cost of Working cover offers. Apart from a clear extension, this concept can also be incorporated into policies arranged on a dual basis (wages). In such an instance, the additional increase in the cost of working would be applied to the wages claim. We will show a typical application in a claims situation in a subsequent chapter. The standard wording is as follows: *"The insurance ... is limited to: The additional expenditure necessarily and reasonably incurred by the insured as a consequence of the incident in order to prevent or minimise the interruption of or interference of the business during the Indemnity Period."*

No underinsurance provisions apply to this cover and it represents a maximum claimable amount (a limit of indemnity). Specialist suppliers, or those dealing with luxury goods, might value their reputation sufficiently that they would wish to spend more money than a particular transaction is worth to ensure that the service to the customer does not suffer. In the case of a retailer, the value of the transaction from a particular member of the public may offer a low economic limit without this policy extension. It should be noted that the Additional Increase in Cost of Working cover is still subject to other aspects of normal increased cost cover.

Additionally, there must still be a benefit produced within the Maximum Indemnity Period.

Costs must still be incurred to mitigate interruption resulting from Damage. The limitations in accepting penalties required under a contract as standard Increased Costs of Working would also be relevant to an Additional Increase in Cost of Working cover. As a general rule, if the insured business has no choice but to incur a cost it is unlikely to be covered under either a Standard Increase in Cost of Working or Additional Increased Cost of Working cover.

Some businesses take the view that Gross Profit cover is not required and arrange business interruption policies with Increase in Cost of Working cover only. Invariably, the claims experience suggests that Gross Profit losses cannot be completely avoided especially for manufacturing companies, however the judicious expenditure of increased costs can mitigate the same. The presumption that a business is sufficiently gifted that any problem can be resolved without any Gross Profit loss arising if only sufficient funds are available to spend has been demonstrated, in the majority of cases, to be wrong. In some cases, businesses cannot incur an increased cost at all.

For example, it might not be possible to subcontract work. Increasingly, the claims experience confirms that the reducing number of businesses operating in various parts of the manufacturing sector is producing difficulty in sourcing subcontractors who are both willing and can take on work in the short to medium-term. Service firms might still be able to operate based on Increase in Cost of Working especially as some services can be provided remotely or from a client's premises.

## 5.1.2 THE SUPPLY CHAIN (CUSTOMERS AND SUPPLIERS EXTENSION)

Incidents occurring at the premises of a supplier or customer can produce just as significant an impact on the insured business as an incident occurring at the Premises. A customer's or supplier's extension provides that loss *"resulting from interruption of or interference with the Business in consequence of loss, destruction or damage at the under noted situations or to properties under noted shall be deemed to be an Incident"* as if it occurred at the

Premises.

The cover will relate either to specific customers/suppliers, or it will be a general cover relating to all customers/suppliers, subject to limits of loss. For specified suppliers/customers the relevant premises will be specifically listed. In the case of the general covers, these relate to *"suppliers, manufacturers or processors of components, goods or materials"* (for suppliers extensions) and for customers with whom there is an existing relationship (i.e. not prospective customers).

There will also be inner limits applicable to the unspecified covers as for the specified customer or supplier extensions. In the case of the latter, specific limits will be selected by the insured business and the premium charged accordingly. In the case of unspecified customers in practice, a 10% limit of the sum insured in any one period would typically apply.

Additionally, it is common practice to find that only a restricted range of insured perils will be provided in relation to the customers'/suppliers' premises. Not all incidents that might be covered at the Premises themselves (under an All Risks cover, for example) would be dealt with if they occurred at the third party sites. There is a requirement for an insured event (loss, destruction or damage) to occur at the suppliers/customers premises giving rise to interruption or interference with the business. General, non-specific interruptions are not covered. Some evidence of the nature of the incident suffered by the customer/supplier will be needed in practice. However, there is no specific requirement for the customer or supplier themselves to have adequate insurance covering the incident or indeed any insurance at all. The insurance arrangements of the customer or supplier are not relevant.

In terms of the operation of the policy, a suppliers extension specifically excludes public utility covers as such extensions are available separately. Some newer services may not be explicitly excluded. Internet service providers, for example, may fall within the definition of suppliers. Whether they do or not, the significance of a website not being available due to an incident at the Internet service provider's premises is one which is just as likely to impact upon the insured business as an incident at the premises of a supplier.

The need for a customers or suppliers extension is generally self-apparent. An over-reliance on any one customer or supplier suggests the need for this cover. Only the insured business is in a position to know that such trading relationships exist. If these are not disclosed to the broker and/or insurer, then avoidable shortfalls in the scope of policy cover may arise.

In practice, there are many situations where claims are not made under unspecified suppliers or customers covers which at face value would be dealt with by the relevant policies if submitted. This might be due to a general lack of awareness of what the policy cover offers and there have been cases where significant incidents have caused the insolvency of suppliers since no orders for raw materials are placed with the supplier until the fire damage is repaired. The supplier may be unable to survive an uninsured but significant loss of turnover.

### 5.1.3 ADVANCE LOSS OF PROFITS

The standard business interruption policy provides cover over a defined period (the Maximum Indemnity Period) commencing from the date of the Damage. This is appropriate for existing income streams but is not so for an income stream which will commence in the future.

A refinery may be arranging for the construction of a new facility or a business may be building a new factory. In either case, Damage to assets will not impact the profit and loss account of the business until the point at which revenue/profit would have started to be generated but for the incident.

This is acknowledged by a revised definition of the indemnity period under an Advance Loss of Profits Cover (as opposed to that in the standard policy wording):

*"The period beginning with the date upon which, but for the Damage, Turnover would have commenced to be earned and ending not later than the Maximum Indemnity Period thereafter during which the results of the business shall be affected in consequence of the Damage."*

It follows that there should be an ascertainable date upon which the profit stream would have occurred but for the Damage. This should, in theory, be easy to establish regarding construction project plans, delivery schedules for plant and equipment etc.

There is another reason for arranging an Advance Loss of Profits Cover in addition to the deferred commencement of loss. The standard cover will operate when there has been Damage to assets owned or used by the insured business for the purpose of that business at the Premises. Where there are assets in the course of construction, these may not have been handed over to the insured business by contractors at the time that they suffer Damage. The business will, therefore, neither own nor use them. Under a standard wording, the Material Damage Proviso will not be satisfied by Damage to assets neither owned nor used for the purpose of the business, and the business interruption cover would not ordinarily be available.

Where there is the addition of two extra machines to a line of twelve existing machines, and where the lead time of purchase is not significant then the standard business interruption cover (assuming an appropriate Maximum Indemnity Period has been selected) is likely to be sufficient. At the other extreme, the construction of a new factory on a new site will certainly require an Advance Loss of Profits Cover. Between these two poles, the situation can be less clear.

Where a business is extending its manufacturing capacity at existing premises, the financial budgets for the coming year will reflect the investment in such assets within the forecast turnover figures. These investments and the additional capacity that they represent would be considered when calculating Standard Turnover for settlement purposes, though the period under consideration would still commence from the date of Damage rather than from the date on which the income stream from the extended capacity would otherwise have commenced.

There is a practical issue to be considered when arranging Advance Loss of Profits Cover and that is the assessment of the insurable amount. Any significant capital expenditure would usually be accompanied by the preparation of a business plan justifying such expenditure in terms of the turnover and profit that will subsequently be generated by it. There can be dissatisfaction on the part of an insured business if the forecast was accepted at face value for premium purposes but is subsequently considered to be an unsatisfactory and unreliable basis to establish quantum if a claim is made.

This contrasts with the majority of claims, where the declaration made at the start of a policy period can be compared to actual (historical) financial performance. With a development that has not yet started, there may be little to support quantum other than the initial forecast. Before arranging Advance Loss of Profits cover and to avoid an expectation difficulty, the insured business should discuss in detail with the insurer/broker the basis of settlement should an insured event occur.

That is not to suggest that forecasts are of no value. For those businesses with a reasonable financial history, it will be possible to validate the accuracy of forecasting and budgeting generally. A parallel situation in terms of assessment of the profitability of a new department can be found with regards to new businesses. The New Business clause acknowledges that a historical financial record may not exist for new businesses suffering insured incidents and in effect accepts that the best estimate, based on what is available, will have to be used in agreeing to a settlement of any claim.

The operation of the Advance Loss of Profits cover follows the standard wording. Standard Turnover reflects the turnover which would have been generated but for the Damage within the Maximum Indemnity Period. As previously noted, that period begins when production would have commenced but for the Damage. The Rate of Gross Profit is the rate that would have been generated within that future period.

There is a slight anomaly when it comes to increased costs. The indemnity period for an Advance Loss of Profits Cover will not commence until the date on which the profit would have begun to have been generated but for the Damage.

If a fire affects assets under construction, there may be a desire to incur additional costs to accelerate repairs so that the commencement of production is as close to the original plan as possible. If these costs are incurred, that would, therefore, be before the commencement of the Maximum Indemnity Period.

Technically, increased costs incurred before the commencement of the indemnity period would not fall for claims consideration. The wording provides no cover for such costs in accelerating repairs to bring the date on which profit begins to be generated back toward the date initially anticipated. Equally, any savings in costs before the initially anticipated commencement date (but for the insured event) would not accrue to insurer's benefit.

In reality, it will be preferable to avoid significant gross profit losses if increased expenditure can be incurred to mitigate them. However, after discussion, even if there is a concession on the part of insurers to deal with increased costs incurred before the commencement of the indemnity period, there will still be a delay whilst the forecast figures are investigated. This will in-

evitably take longer than assessing Standard Turnover under a claim at the Premises due to the absence of historical trade figures relating to the
the new element of the business.

The need for the insured business to communicate, as rapidly as possible, any proposed mitigation plan to allow the merits to be considered is, therefore, significant. It can be a good idea to discuss with the insured business (at the time that an Advance Loss of Profits Cover is being arranged) whether any additional costs could be expended if an incident were to occur, and if so, what sort of cost is envisaged. Discussion can then take place with the insurers to avoid misunderstandings at claims time and to establish that there is consistency in intent as to what the cover is addressing between the insured business and the insurer.

## Rating of Advance Loss of Profits

Rating for advance loss of profits depends on the complexity of the work and the length of the contract. The longer the time until handover of the construction the more time is available to repair damage to reduce delay and any consequent loss of profit. All risks cover is standard, made up of fire, dry perils, wet perils and accidental damage rates.

**Illustration of possible Advance Loss of Profits Rates**

| Period | Fire: complexity of construction A | B | C | Dry Perils | Wet Perils and AD |
|---|---|---|---|---|---|
| 0 - 6 months | .15% | .20% | .25% | .030% | .080% |
| 6 - 12 months | .125% | .135% | .20% | .027% | .072% |
| 12 – 18 months | .10% | .120% | .140% | .020% | .050% |

Fire rates are graded according to the complexity and fire potential of the construction. In reality, insurers may wish to have several different grades of construction complexity in their rating tables. The fire (and sometimes, explosion) rates are highest because there is a possibility of a large damage loss and a relatively long delay period whereas perils rates are lower because actual damage losses are likely to be smaller and be repaired more quickly, thus causing less delay to the project/programme.

### 5.1.4 UTILITY EXTENSIONS

The Utility Extensions available expand the cover to deal with incidents away from the Premises and also in effect extend the range of perils. There are two distinct extensions available to insure utilities.

**The first extension** covers loss (as insured by the policy) resulting from loss, destruction or Damage at the land-based Premises of utility suppliers, be that an electricity, gas, water or telecommunications business. This extension requires an incident to occur at the premises of utility providers and will require Damage to occur there which causes the failure in supply.

In practical terms, it is very unusual for claims to be paid under this particular extension. This is partly because supply can be re-routed by the utility company, to some extent, following any failure at land-based premises. More importantly, the majority of utility failure occurs because of an incident in between the generating station and the insured's Premises, affecting the cabling, for example, as far as communication, electricity, etc. is concerned. It is relevant to note that the term 'Premises' has been held to include inspection pits set in the pavements to allow access to gas/electric installations and that cover is, therefore, wider than if it related just to those demised Premises on which buildings stand.

**The second type of utility extension** covers interruption or interference with the business due to accidental failure of the utility (electricity/gas/water/telecommunications) at the point of supply at the premises of the insured business. This will be the main stop cock in the case of water, the supply authority's meter in the case of power or gas.

Accidental damage to cabling particularly near railways, construction areas or canals is common. The overwhelming majority of utility claims are dealt with under this latter extension. If an insured business identifies the need for cover in relation to the failure of a utility, this will most effectively be achieved through this extension rather than the alternative covering the premises of the supply authority only.

It is worth noting that there are defined points in the supply cabling/pipework, before which the incident must occur for cover under this extension to be available. The logic of this is that if there is damage beyond those points they would comprise property for which the insured is responsible and would generate a standard material damage claim which would, in turn, satisfy the Material Damage Proviso and allow a 'normal' business interruption claim to be made.

There may be a time excess or franchise. Short Maximum Indemnity Periods will commonly be arranged compared to the main perils of fire, flood etc. Such shorter periods acknowledge that interruptions in utility supply will usually be of very limited duration (the current situation in Nigeria is not ideal). Business interruption losses will generally be more limited than those arising from fires or floods.

It is worthwhile noting that there are significant exclusions particular to the utility extensions, most notably any deliberate act of the supply authority. Failure at the terminal ends will not be covered if the electricity company, for example, isolated supply to allow necessary work to take place. Finally, it should be noted that the utility extensions extend the business interruption and not the material damage cover. Spoilage of stock and work in progress following a power failure would not be claimable under this extension, though it could be addressed separately as part of the material damage section of the policy. This is consistent with stock spoilage arising after fire or flood, for example.

## 5.1.5 DENIAL, PREVENTION AND HINDRANCE OF ACCESS

The standard wording is as follows:

*"Property in the vicinity of the Premises, loss or destruction of or damage to which shall prevent or hinder the use of the Premises or access thereto, whether the Premises or property of the insured therein shall be damaged or not, but excluding loss or destruction of or damage to property of any supply undertaking from which the insured obtains electricity, gas, water or telecommunication services which prevents or hinders the supply of such services, to the premises."*

There is a requirement for a specific event to have occurred and for damage to have affected property in the vicinity. There is no cover for contractors carrying out maintenance work on roads or utilities in the vicinity, or access restrictions having been granted by the local authority to allow for adjacent construction work, for example.

Some package policies available provide Denial of Access Cover as a matter of course, extending the cover from the standard cover, which requires damage at the premises, to business interruption claims following damage at or near the premises. The term vicinity is undefined, but a potential radius from the premises of as much as twenty-five miles can be inferred from case law. The issue is the extent to which a direct link can be established between the location of damage and the Premises rather than a strict distance between the two.

Whilst this extension is often referred to as the denial or prevention of access, the cover is more extensive than that, allowing for hindrance of the use of the premises or access thereto. A hindrance is not qualified or quantified nor is there a differentiation between the vehicle or pedestrian use. A hindrance resulting from damage in the vicinity will, therefore, trigger the cover just as much as a total denial. (It would still be necessary to be able to demonstrate that any depression in trading figures could be related to the hindrance. In the same way, that satisfaction of the Material Damage Proviso will not allow a claim for loss not flowing from Damage to succeed, there must still be a causative effect. The identification of some form of hindrance will not in itself allow a claim for all and any variation in the business subsequent to that event.) Sometimes, it can be difficult to conclude that a hindrance has occurred or continues to occur.

Traditionally, the extension related to damage in the vicinity, although more recently, non-damage extensions have become available, for example when the competent authority denies the use of a road leading to the Insured Premises. This extension acknowledges that, while an incident in the vicinity of the Insured Premises would not satisfy the material damage proviso, it could still severely affect the business and result in a reduction in Turnover. The cover is provided for denial/prevention or hindrance of access to Insured Premises, but not egress from them.

The problem is that keywords in a typical extension are not usually clearly defined, for example, 'vicinity', 'damage', or 'hinder'. Dictionary definitions are insufficient to provide certainty of cover. There is no reference point for the degree of disruption required to satisfy the policy requirements. For example, vehicular access may be impacted differently to pedestrian access. Again, it is unclear as to whether hindrance may only be construed in a physical way, such that disruption to the Internet or telecommunication networks is not covered by such an extension.

In some cases, the (undefined) damage denying/hindering access is very close to the insured Premises, for example, next door. Difficulties arise though when there is clear evidence of denial/hindrance resulting from damage at more distant locations. Where 'vicinity' is specified as a discreet distance, there remains uncertainty as to how this should be measured for example, as the crow flies, or by road or rail routes. The extension, by not using the defined term 'Damage', and instead using the word damage in an everyday sense (without a capital letter), potentially provides cover for a wider range of losses than are insured at the

Premises themselves. In the absence of a definition, expectations between the parties often vary widely. Consequently, inconsistencies arise.

To the extent that it is intended for this extension to cover egress as well as access, wordings could be amended to say so specifically. Concerning the key terms discussed above: It might be attractive to define 'vicinity' as a specified distance from the insured Premises. However, this would potentially give rise to several issues, for example:

- the methodology of measurement;
- the problem of adjacent businesses that suffer equally, being treated differently if one is just within the measurement and the other not;
- the coverage position may still be unclear if part of the insured Premises falls within the specified distance, but the access/egress points fall outside it.

Consequently, while specifying a distance may resolve some uncertainties, it may create others. Therefore, not defining the term 'vicinity' remains a viable option, accepting that each claim will need to be treated on its merits.

### 5.1.6 LOSS OF ATTRACTION

A standard wording will deal with interruption to and interference with the business in relation to *'Property in the vicinity of the Premises, destruction of or damage to which will cause loss of custom to the insured directly due to loss of amenities in the immediate vicinity of the Premises whether the Premises or property of the insured therein shall be damaged or not'.*

This cover will be highly relevant where a business relies on the presence of neighbouring facilities to generate its income. Restaurants located next to hotels and cinema can rely on the latter for much of their income. Shops can enjoy passing trade because of the presence of a major retail chain. Cafés may be supported by the business of employees of a major local manufacturer. In these cases, the absence of the source of attraction could produce losses as significant as Damage at the Premises themselves and the need for this extension should be seriously considered. As with the denial/prevention of access cover, 'vicinity' is not defined, although the word 'immediate' is placed before it in this wording.

Whilst that still does not quantify the term, it suggests an intention to restrict the scope of cover compared to the Denial of Access extension. In arranging a loss of attraction cover the insured business would almost certainly have identified the attraction that it is seeking cover against and, to avoid any misunderstanding, this can be specifically identified to insurers with its proximity clearly stated to avoid any difficulty at claims time.

CHAPTER 6:
# POLICY DESIGN AND EXTENSIONS – PART 2

## 6.1 ENGINEERING POLICIES

An engineering policy offers three heads of cover, being: Breakdown, Accidental Damage and Loss of Utilities.

### 1. Breakdown

The desire for breakdown cover is invariably the main reason for the engineering policy being incepted. The breakdown would not be covered under a standard policy wording; it would simply not constitute an insured event of loss or Damage.

Breakdown cover is not a replacement for a proper maintenance program. Gradually operating causes and wear and tear issues will be excluded. It should be noted that there is a need to not only carry out the maintenance but to evidence the same. A failure to do so can produce difficulty if the nature of a breakdown is uncertain. The evidence of a planned maintenance regime can bring clarity and assist prompt resolution of a claim.

### 2. Accidental Damage

The type of incident which will give rise to a claim under the Accidental Damage cover would already be dealt with by an All Risks policy. The need for accidental damage is therefore likely only to be necessary if the commercial combined policy has been written on a Perils rather than on an All Risks basis.

The cover relates to sudden and unforeseen Damage arising from an accidental cause. Gradually arising causes and wear and tear are again excluded. It should also be noted that the cover relates to the plant at the Premises. A separate transit cover would need to be arranged if the plant was being moved. In the past, significant Damage has been caused to plant taken off-site for maintenance. Such damage, not occurring at the Premises, is not covered.

## 3. Utilities

Utility extensions are available as part of the general cover, as has been previously discussed. The availability of utility cover under an engineering policy allows the extension to be related to a specific machine rather than the Premises generally, which may sometimes provide a premium advantage. Relating the cover to specific machines will also be the case with regards to breakdown and accidental damage. These relate to specific pieces of the plant rather than being a general floating cover over the whole of the plant and equipment of the Premises.

There are two specific aspects of Engineering policies that are not found under standard covers. Firstly, Maximum Indemnity Periods are often very much shorter than for the core policy. Three months would be typical, with a range of between one and six months commonly taken out. The logic of a three month Maximum Indemnity Period for breakdown compared to a much longer period for Damage caused by fire, for example, acknowledges the potentially wider scope of damage that the latter might represent.

There is also an assumption, however, that Damage to a specific machine can be repaired more easily and quickly than general fire or flood damage. This was certainly the case historically when manufacturing businesses employed maintenance staff who would be able to provide labour and the expertise to effect repairs. The need to obtain spare parts was the only cause of delay. These days in many industries, given that plant and equipment has become increasingly sophisticated, that scope for internal maintenance can be limited and suppliers need to be relied upon. There may be limited availability of spare parts, and also a need to wait for a machine supplier's specialist labour to install the same when they are available. The impact of these factors is that the need for an appropriately long Maximum Indemnity Period under an Engineering policy is just as important as for a general commercial combined policy. Three month periods are increasingly proving to be insufficient.

Secondly, the engineering policy cover typically incorporates an excess period in terms of time rather than a finite monetary amount. (This may be a franchise rather than an excess whereby the whole of the loss is payable if the stated time is exceeded without any deduction, whereas an excess will be deducted regardless of the duration of the incident.) It is not usually explicitly stated whether the period of excess/franchise commences with the occurrence of the Damage or with the occurrence of the business interruption loss.

Consider an incident occurring at 5.00 pm on a Friday for a business which does not commonly work weekends. If there is a forty-eight hour excess period, in chronological terms, that period expired over the Saturday/Sunday when no production would have taken place regardless of the incident. The policy wording should be taken at face value and using an everyday interpretation of the wording unless there is ambiguity or a specific need to do otherwise. A forty-eight-hour excess, therefore, should run chronologically from the point of the damage in the same way as a Maximum Indemnity Period commences from the point of the Damage.

There might be a temptation, following an incident, for increased costs to be deferred until after an excess period has expired. This does not avoid the application of the excess. If gross profit losses immediately after an incident are not payable because of a time excess, any increased costs incurred (at any time) to avoid such losses would by definition be uneconomic. It is the timing of the gross profit loss that is important, not the timing of the increased costs. As a corollary, increased costs incurred within an excess period to mitigate gross profit losses thereafter would be payable.

It should be noted that this cover is a business interruption cover and following a breakdown, as with a cessation of electric supply under a utility extension, any spoilage of stock in the process will not give rise to a payment relating to the stock itself. Solidification of plastic pellets within an extrusion line could be a problem, as could solidification of metal in casting pots or moulds. Such material damage wastage is not covered.

Finally, there is the issue of concurrent causes of loss. If a machine head crashes due to wear and tear failure of a ball bearing there may be subsequent impact damage on the machine bed. Subsequent impact damage would be insured but the wear and tear failure would be excluded. In the majority of situations, the insured cause runs beyond and overrides the excluded cause such that the whole loss will be payable. There are occasions, however, where replacement of the part suffering the wear and tear failure has taken longer than the repair of the insured damage. In such a situation the exclusion would override entirely giving rise to no payment being due from insurers.

## 6.2 FINES & PENALTIES

In certain trades, the delivery of goods to the customer by the due date is a very important feature and in the contract of sale or services, a provision is made for the payment of a fine or damages in the event of non-fulfilment by the agreed date. Although a loss of this nature may be a consequence of damage, it is normally excluded from the cover (liquidated damages.).

This position often applies in sections of the engineering, printing, textiles, clothing and similar industries, in building construction and in certain government contracts. Where there is a liability of this kind and there is no 'force majeure' clause in the contract providing for its cancellation in the event of a fire or other perils under an insured's policy or even damage beyond the insured's control, it is possible to arrange a special sub limited item on fines or damages for breach of contract.

The sum insured for such an item is calculated on a first loss basis and should represent the maximum liability that might arise at any one point of time from anyone particular incident. In estimating what this loss might be, allowance can be made for the possibility of getting work done by other firms in order to fulfil contracts. The additional cost of doing so will be met under the increase in cost of working section of the insurance on gross profit/revenue within the terms and limitations of that section because it will produce turnover which otherwise would have been lost. In the reverse direction, cover can be expanded to include fines or damages, etc. which the insured shall be legally liable to pay, for breach of contract. This would arise in consequence of the damage in respect of contracts for the purchase of goods or services that cannot be utilised by the business during the indemnity period.

A payment which has to be made to a customer because of a historic contract would not, as has been previously observed, fall for consideration as an Increased Cost of Working. It would be incurred primarily because of a historic contract and not solely to avoid a future reduction in turnover. Neither would it be covered as an Additional Increase in Cost of Working. It would not be reasonably and necessarily incurred to avoid future interruption to the business but, again, because of the existence of the historic contract.

If it is the intention to insure against contractual penalties then a fines and penalties extension will have to be added to the policy. This item will be subject to a separate Limit of Indemnity relating to payments which are legally liable to be paid for any breach of contract in consequence of an incident.

The level of indemnity will, by definition, be dictated by the largest contractual exposure with a customer. The insured business should be able to establish this without difficulty and premium quotations can be obtained. The economics of insuring or dealing with the risk any other way can then be considered.

In the absence of formal written contracts, it may still be the case that the custom and practice of a particular industry does entail payments to customers where disruption is caused to them, whether by an event insured or not. In that situation, the penalty payments would be a contractual matter although not one evidenced in writing. This may be the case with supermarkets who may demand payments representing the profit that they would have been achieved on the sale of the product on the shelves (notwithstanding that other product would have filled the shelf space and generated alternative profit). Whilst such claims could be resisted both on liability and quantum grounds, contractual payments may still have to be made if that is the custom.

## 6.3 RESEARCH & DEVELOPMENT

Research often represents the investigation or application of new technologies, or qualities of materials, or general experimentation, with broad objectives which, if met, would allow further investigatory work to be undertaken. That is to be contrasted with development work which is generally intended to apply the generic research and develop specific new products for sale.

Where the development period is relatively short, and where the Maximum Indemnity Period is appropriately long, Damage which affects the project at the Premises may be largely covered under the existing Gross Profit cover development costs are unlikely to be have been uninsured.

If development work is subcontracted to third party premises, in whole or in part, then an incident could occur there which would not trigger policy cover as the Material Damage Proviso might not be satisfied. From the point of view of the insured business that would most ideally be covered by extending the definition of premises though at the expense of a reduced range of perils and subject to an inner limit.

Research has a less direct focus and, in common with longer product development periods, ongoing research may not give rise to turnover generation potentially for years. Damage affecting the research assets is, therefore, unlikely to produce a reduction in turnover or any payment under the Gross Profit item. If no Gross Profit is at risk, then by definition no increased costs could be paid as they would automatically be uneconomic.

To address this, a separate item with a limit of indemnity could be arranged in respect of research and development which would typically pay a pro-rata proportion of the annual research and expenditure cost every week, subject to a Maximum Indemnity Period. The cover would allow for the recreation of research that has been lost and which has to be recreated.

In those situations where the research represents the creation of data which itself is properly backed up and saved off-site then the need for recreation may be reduced. Ongoing laboratory testing could be lost as could hard copy statistical surveys or analysis. The ease of replacement of both information gained from research and of the assets used in the research department generally will dictate the need for this extension.

The difficulty has been experienced in the past in replacing sophisticated laser and other electronic systems for which there can be lead times of many months. In the case of universities, damage to research equipment may require the recreation of work already undertaken (particularly if a repeat of any earlier trials is necessary to comply with proper validation or quality control). However, there is also an income issue if grants are received to support the education of students in the relevant department, or where commercial sponsorship might be jeopardised if the research is interrupted.

It is recommended that the time scale for the replacement of significant pieces of plant in a research department is considered in precisely the same way as for production departments. The ease of replacement of data developed should also be discussed and the existence of any income streams which might be jeopardised properly identified.

The latter would not be addressed through a standard research and development wording, which offers support for costs incurred but not for any ongoing loss of income. It could be appropriate to include any such grants or sponsorship monies within the definition of turnover, slightly altering the standard wording to ensure that there is no shortfall at claims time.

## 6.4 OUTBREAK OF NOTIFIABLE DISEASE

This extension provides cover for any *'loss resulting from interruption of or interference with the Business carried on by the insured at the Premises'* in respect of:

1) An outbreak of a notifiable disease at the Premises/within twenty-five miles of the Premises, or of the discovery of an organism likely to give rise to such a disease.

2) The discovery of vermin/pests at the Premises causing a restriction on the order or advice of a local authority.

3) An accident or defect in the drains causing restrictions on the order of a local authority.

4) The occurrence of murder/suicide at the Premises.

Hotels, cafés and restaurants need such cover as do schools, hospitals and leisure centres/swimming pools. On a much wider basis, any business involved with the production or distribution of food should give careful consideration to the need to extend the basic policy wording in this way.

There are defined lists of diseases in respect of which local authorities can act and it should be noted that only the diseases falling into those categories would trigger policy cover. Where local authorities extend their power and restrict the activities of a business in respect of a non-notifiable disease. A compliant business may then seek reimbursement of losses from insurers, only to find that cover is unavailable. A clear understanding of the scope and limitations of the cover at inception is essential. Non-notifiable diseases, such as Norovirus, or bird flu can give rise to significant business interruption that may not be covered by the policy wording.

With regards to notifiable disease, the standard Association of British Insurers (ABI) wording refers to *'any human infectious or human contagious disease'* (excluding Aids) rather than a disease in any form. This distinction became important following the outbreak of 'mad cow' disease in the past, which was a notifiable disease, but not one that related to humans. Not all policy wordings followed the ABI standard, and some policies inadvertently gave cover for claims arising from an outbreak of a notifiable disease affecting animals.

In the majority of cases, no business interruption loss could be claimed, as the losses arising did not derive from the outbreak of a notifiable disease a few miles from a particular restaurant, but rather from the fact that customers were largely avoiding rural areas, as invited to do at the time by the authorities.

The Maximum Indemnity Period can be defined by the insured business. In respect of the four aspects of cover listed above, the commencement of that period is explicitly set out. It will commence once any notifiable disease has been discovered or a murder/suicide has occurred. The cover in respect of vermin and problems with the drains allows for the indemnity period to commence when restrictions imposed by a local authority come into force.

With regards to the sanitary arrangements/drains, blockages would not comprise accidents - specific extraneous incidents must occur. In many cases, accidental damage to drains is repairable reasonably quickly and the duty to mitigate loss applies as with any other cover. Again, this is a business interruption extension and the cost of repairing the damage would not, therefore, fall for consideration.

The recent wave of diseases such as Coronavirus, Ebola, etc. would mean that insurers granting this cover may be selective in terms of locations and limits in order to reduce their exposure. Clients, on the other hand, will be desirous of this cover as the impact on business can be massive. The situation with Coronavirus as at August 2020 is still evolving but the worldwide impact is already devastating as WHO (World Health Organisation) had declared a global pandemic as far back as February 2020. Pandemics and in particular Covid-19 is discussed separately in chapter 11 of this book.

## 6.5 ATTEMPTED MURDER/SUICIDE

Murder/suicide at the Premises can give rise to a significant reduction in the level of turnover, where this produces a disinclination for other guests to stay at a hotel, for example. Certain hotels see reasonably high levels of suicide, selected on the basis that they can be relied upon to deal with the matter in a dignified and discreet way.

Two issues are worth raising. Firstly, the definition of Premises is important. A claim was brought on one occasion by a bakery concession in a cut-price supermarket. Without any prior warning, one of the employees of the supermarket attacked several customers and colleagues with a machete. Some two months later one of the customers that had been badly injured died, and there was understandably a depression in turnover in the immediate aftermath, causing significant cash flow hardship to the concession.

The initial consideration was the definition of Premises - did these comprise merely the area occupied by the concession or the whole supermarket? It was decided that the Premises related to the whole demised building, although that conclusion was not inevitable at the time. The uncertainty that arose whilst the matter was resolved was unsettling for the insured business. Clarification of the definition of Premises in advance would have assisted.

Secondly, the cover specifically relates to murder or suicide. Continuing the example quoted above, when the case of the machete-wielding employee went to trial, because the mental health of the individual was deemed to be poor, and it was not considered that he fully understood what he was doing, he was found guilty of manslaughter on the basis of diminished responsibility.

This conclusion of the court was not available for a significant period after the bakery concession claim was concluded. Manslaughter is not an incident triggering cover and consideration was given to the recovery of funds from the insured person which initially were released on the assumption of murder. No action aimed at securing repayment was ultimately taken, but it emphasises that there might be uncertainty as to whether an event constitutes murder or not. The confirmation of an indemnity under this extension can be significantly delayed pending police investigation and the insured business must be prepared to fulfil its obligation to mitigate loss in the interim.

## 6.6 LOSS OF LICENCE/FRANCHISE

There are a variety of different covers available under this broad heading, the commercial wordings varying significantly. Following significant damage to a tenanted public house, the brewery (or relevant building owner) may decide not to reinstate the damage but to sell the premises on. They may decide to alter the use of the building, for example, introducing restaurant facilities where none existed before. They may reinstate a public house, but one with significantly different décor and aiming for a significantly different market than before, perhaps with an aspiration to alter the tenant.

This places the insured tenant in a very difficult position. Assuming that an adequate core business interruption policy has been arranged, any loss of profit during the Maximum Indemnity Period will be covered. Tenants will often live above the public house that they manage and their need to attend to their personal situation and the domestic insurance claim alongside the commercial business is a significant issue.

The tenant in this position is likely to have even less control over the building repair programme that would normally be the case for restaurants, clubs and bars will be more sensitive to changing moods and fashions in terms of fixtures and fittings, even more than a retailer (fashion changes will initially impact on stock ranges for them). The possibility of an extended period of downtime presents itself whilst all options are considered.

These covers, therefore, anticipate that trading may not have recommenced by the end of the Maximum Indemnity Period and that there may be an ongoing loss. In a departure from the normal situation where only losses within the Maximum Indemnity Period will be considered, the loss of license wordings allows for the value of the lost license beyond the end of the Maximum Indemnity Period.

There are a wider variety of issues to consider in calculating such ongoing loss compared to trading losses within a fixed period and there is the issue of what else the insured person is doing into the future. As a consequence, these claims might not be resolved until sometime after an incident, and cash flow hardship may result. This is an unavoidable consequence of all relevant factors having to be considered. An awareness that interim payments that might be made during the life of a normal business interruption policy within the Maximum Indemnity Period could be more difficult to make before resolution of a loss of license claim can avoid expectation difficulties.

Franchisees face similar if not identical problems. In the case of fast food outlets, many franchisees will own all of the assets generating sales and will, therefore, be in control of the repair period. Even so, there may be restrictions in franchise agreements that require stringent performance and which may not allow undue delay in sourcing replacement quotations. This is likely to place particular pressure on material damage sums insured (marginal underinsurance might otherwise be addressed by a longer tendering period). Involuntary betterment might arise by having to comply with ongoing franchisor specification improvements, producing additional pressure on the resources of the insured business. It might be the case, however, that the franchise agreement allows the franchisor a terminal option if there is a cessation of supply for stipulated periods. In considering the need for any extension to the basic cover, the franchise agreement should be carefully considered to identify any such issues. It will be appreciated that the franchisee who does not own all of the assets is at greater risk following significant damage in the same way as a tenant.

The existence and availability of this type of insurance recognise that license holders or franchisees are at risk of not having long-term participation in the brand which underpins their business. The much stronger hand in post-loss decision making is likely to rest with the franchisor or other relevant business.

For a normal commercial business which has created its brand, it would not be appropriate to provide cover for ongoing losses after the end of the Maximum Indemnity Period on the basis that such businesses do have the opportunity to mitigate losses and to directly control the mitigation strategy. As they have the ability to do so, it is equitable that they should carry the risk of success or failure.

Business interruption insurance concerns itself with pecuniary loss rather than the inconvenience and general compensation payment for the future would be inconsistent with that. A normal commercial business which has more direct control over its own destiny is able to protect itself through the selection of an appropriately long Maximum Indemnity Period. Whilst there is an increasing focus on brand damage and ongoing tarnishment to reputation, brand damage at the end of the day reveals itself in reduced sales.

There are two final observations to make. Firstly, a franchisee will be required under any of the relevant wordings to demonstrate that every possible effort has been made to mitigate the loss arising and to secure an ongoing license/franchise to mitigate a loss as would normally be expected. Any failure to do so will invalidate a claim under this head of the cover. There is a need to work very closely with the insurer/loss adjuster so that difficulties are identified at the earliest possible time and to give everybody an opportunity of influencing the outcome is essential.

Secondly, it may be that the franchisor will arrange insurance cover for the convenience of franchisees generally, and also so that he knows that they are adequately insured and have not overlooked the need to set-up relevant policies. Whilst such support may be very welcome, it is in the franchisor's interest to ensure that such appropriate policies are taken out. Inevitably, care will have been taken to ensure that primarily his position is protected rather than necessarily taking the position of the franchisee into consideration in the first instance. The appropriateness of such cover should be carefully considered with this in mind.

## 6.7 CONTINGENCY COVERS

There are certain businesses, notably including those which organise annual trade shows or events, that may not own the building in which their exhibition is to take place but which are at risk of something occurring either there or elsewhere which would provide a reluctance for the public to visit.

Whilst it would be possible to consider altering the standard wording to provide cover following Damage at the exhibition location, the threat to income, which significantly presents itself off-site, would still remain. This risk primarily relates to attendance by the public. Trade attendance, where there is a business imperative involved, is less at risk.

A contingency cover acknowledges this and allows for the occurrence of events (undefined) which caused a significant number of attendees in the light of such an event to not take part in the exhibition/show. Attendance fees would drop and there could be a significant loss of income. The requirement (wordings vary) will be for widespread impact of an event not necessarily in one specific region but relating to the country generally. Examples would include the stationing of the military around a major airport, a major road/rail disaster, air crash or some similar occurrence. Strike action, or the deliberate act of any supply undertaking, will often be exclusions, though not universally so.

There can be difficulties in establishing quantum where there are large annual events particularly if there is significant variation in the financial results historically. Similar observations apply to those made in respect of Advanced Profits cover above. The extent to which the Gross Profit or Revenue that the cover is being arranged to protect can be audited is a significant issue. If an insured business is unable to at least provide detailed budgets, supplying further supporting documentation if required, this will speak to the ease with which quantum can be demonstrated if a claim were to be made.

Businesses become agitated if a budget was accepted at face value for the calculation of premium, but is considered insufficient to support quantum when a claim is made. The perception is unreasonable. Insurers cannot bear the cost of investigating budgets and forecasts regardless of claims arising, as that would have to be reflected in the premium.

In the past and with insurers approval, loss adjusters have investigated quantum in advance of any claim, and have confirmed the reasonableness of budgets (or otherwise) with the cost of them so doing paid by the client. This can be accompanied by an agreement that the element of the loss adjuster's costs that would have been required when a claim is made will then be dealt with by the insurer, via a repayment to the client.

It is, of course, difficult to suggest to an insured business that further outlays be paid on top of what might be perceived as a significant premium. Notwithstanding that, there are businesses taking out contingency covers that have an extremely low ability to demonstrate and prove quantum should a claim be made. It is suggested that the ability to evidence quantum should be properly considered at the time the policy cover is incepted. If there will be a significant difficulty, this should be discussed in some detail beforehand. Insurers can only reasonably be expected to make payments if quantum can be verified. It may be that contingency covers will not be the best way to manage risk if quantum will be unduly subjective.

Whilst the discussion of contingency covers has been framed within the context of exhibitions/events, the range of incidences that such cover might be relevant to is very wide. Related cover, for example, deals with non-appearance or cancellation of celebrity attendance at events. In those cases where the cover deals with reimbursement of the cost involved and where the costs can be separately identified, then a lot of the difficulties anticipated in the preceding paragraphs will not arise. Regardless of the precise nature of the contingency, the ability to evidence loss were a claim to be made will often help dictate how the cover is incepted and designed.

There can be difficulty in applying those covers which settle claims on the basis of cost rather than profit or revenue. In the vast majority of cases, the cost of putting on an event, from a village fête to a major sporting event, will be fixed. To the extent that part of the whole of the event cannot be run, those costs relating to that part of the event will have been wasted. The policy reimburses historically incurred, but wasted costs rather than additional costs to avoid loss.

## 6.8 ALIEN ABDUCTION, ETC.

Almost anything can be insured as long as it is fortuitous and for an appropriate premium. It has been possible to buy policies in respect of the risk of abduction by aliens among other things in some part of the world. To satisfy Corporate Governance requirements, mere consideration of a risk, with a conclusion that it cannot economically be dealt with, is sufficient for the directors of the business to discharge their duties.

The fact that it is difficult to consider many more extensions that would in real life be of practical use is a compliment to the core policy wording. Whilst the wording is often criticised as being too generic, that is its virtue not its vice. That there are relatively few extensions that need to be considered confirms that.

## CHAPTER 7
## CLAUSES CLARIFYING THE CORE COVER

There are several clauses and covers that apply to commercial policies whether explicitly stated on the face of the policy or not. Such clauses are essentially confirming (existing) aspects of indemnity, and are, therefore, not extending the cover, but they nevertheless provide reassurance to the insured business with regards the policy response in specific situations. The main clauses falling into this category are as follows.

### 7.1 OTHER CIRCUMSTANCES (BUSINESS CIRCUMSTANCES) CLAUSE

In defining the business interruption cover, most policies will define the terms Rate of Gross Profit, Annual Turnover and Standard Turnover to the left-hand side of one of the pages in the policy, with a large bracket relating these three definitions to a paragraph to the right. That paragraph will essentially allow for any of the three terms to be varied as necessary such that the anticipated financial result most closely resembles what would have occurred but for the incident. Whilst that paragraph has no formal title, it is referred to as the other circumstances or any circumstances clause, as it allows for any circumstances generally that would have affected the business but for an incident to be taken into account in calculating loss.

With regards the Rate of Gross Profit, there has been debate as to whether the other circumstances clause allows companies to claim specific rates of gross profit for particular segments of their business in the absence of a departmental clause on the face of the policy. There is technical merit in this argument, in that the other circumstances clause relates to the Rate (singular) of Gross Profit rather than Rates (plural) of Gross Profit.

However, the use of rates specific to departments may pro-

duce a better quantification of the extent of the loss rather than one overall rate. Accordingly, the Association of British Insurers accept (as set out in the Recommended Practices, Wordings and Procedures Manual) that the other circumstances clause specifically includes the following three clauses, regardless of whether they appear on the face of the policy or not:
- Departmental Clause
- New Business Clause
- Salvage Sale Clause

In Nigerian practice, it is safe to say that the above situation holds. However, for the sake of contract certainty, it is often best to state the clauses on the face of the policy. The cover normally available under those clauses is not extended. There are limitations in respect of the application of those clauses and such limitations would apply just as much if they are imported by the other circumstances clause as if they were printed on the face of the policy itself.

## 7.2 ALTERNATIVE TRADING CLAUSE

The alternative trading clause stipulates that, if any turnover that would have been generated from the Premises which suffer an incident, has been generated elsewhere, then such turnover generated elsewhere will be treated as actual turnover in calculating any shortfall payable by the policy.

It is useful to clarify this point, as the policy will only deal with loss at the Premises. The addition of the alternative trading clause avoids an insured business mistakenly assuming that actual turnover generated elsewhere might, therefore, be omitted from the calculations of loss. Most insured businesses will accept that additional turnover generated elsewhere, which would not have been generated but for the incident, should be deducted from anticipated turnover in calculating a loss, in the same way as actual turnover generated normally.

It is tempting to think of the application of the alternative trading clause in terms of a business relocating to brand new premises after the occurrence of an incident. That is not the only situation where the alternative trading clause could apply. If a business has several depots, it may be possible to redirect business to one of the other depots or to service customers therefrom at an Increased Cost. Increased turnover at other existing premises is, therefore, also brought within the ambit of the cover.

## 7.3 NEW BUSINESS CLAUSE

The new business clause acknowledges that the standard wording will not apply to a business that does not have a trading history. It will be recalled that Standard Turnover is defined as the turnover in the preceding year over the period which corresponds with the indemnity period post incident. In other words, an incident occurring in January 2020 which affected a business for January, February and March would have a standard turnover initially based on the period January to March inclusive in 2019.

If a business only commenced trading at the beginning of January 2020, then the turnover in the preceding year will be Nil as it did not exist. To avoid anybody concluding that Standard Turnover should be taken as Nil (and that there is, therefore, no loss), the New Business Clause clarifies the equitable position, which is that best estimates will be made to establish
what the turnover would have been but for the incident.

In practice, many businesses will rely on new finance at inception and a business plan may have been prepared to support such borrowing which would act as an initial starting point in estimating what would have occurred but for the incident. Hopefully, that same business plan will have been used as a basis for calculating the insurable gross profit for policy declaration purposes. Difficulties can arise if the documentation submitted to support a claim is inconsistent with that used to calculate the insurable amount at inception/renewal.

Of course, the existence of a business plan reflects anticipation and is not a guarantee that what was anticipated would have come to pass. This can be augmented by any production plans that may be available and there is likely to be some actual trading history (though over a short period) which may speak to the accuracy of the forecast. Alternatively, it may be that a history of forecasting in respect of other businesses (were it to be a group policy, for example) could assist. The extent to which expenses have been incurred is again an indicator of the turnover anticipation.

No special action is required in respect of the new business clause - it is a clarification of the reality of working with what evidence exists if an incident occurs shortly after opening. Notwithstanding that, the onus to prove and quantify a loss remains with the insured business.

## 7.4 PROFESSIONAL ACCOUNTANTS CLAUSE

Many policies automatically include a professional accountants clause. This clause will be of particular assistance to an insured with limited resource in the administration and finance departments. The professional accountants clause caters for requests from insurers for further documentation and analysis necessary to allow proper consideration of a claim, by providing cover for the costs charged by professional accountants to produce such information.

The cover only relates to further work requested in writing by insurers or their representatives (generally loss adjusters) and would not cover costs arising from work which accountants of an insured business thought would be a good idea at their own initiative.

Likewise, this clause does not provide any cover for the initial calculation of a claim and relates to further information required by insurers. The policy will explicitly confirm that the insured have to submit a claim at their own expense. They can, of course, be assisted by their accountants in that process, but the costs thereof would not be covered.

To avoid confusion, where the accountants are retained to do work, as well setting out the scope of the exercise in writing, it is a good idea to ask the accountants to provide an indicative budget and to provide an early opportunity for review if the cost of the exercise proves to exceed that budget. Avoidable complications arise where budget indications are given, the work is done and very significantly higher costs are then submitted to the business as a fait accompli.

A further point to appreciate is that this cover does not allow any random firm of accountants to be used, but will relate to the accountants acting regularly for the insured business before the incident. A business using the services of a local bookkeeper would not be at liberty to involve one of the large firms of chartered accountants as a special matter for the insurance claim. On the other hand, if one of the large firms of accountants work for the insured business as a matter of course, then it is quite reasonable to allow them to also use that firm for the analysis required.

The cost of the work undertaken by the accountant should reflect the fee structure normally applying to work done for the insured business. Special rates for the claim are inappropriate.

This cover is not intended to pay for the production of information which is readily available to the insured business. For example, a request for a schedule of turnover by month over three years prior to an incident reflects a request for information readily available to the insured business. Mindful of the common law and policy duty to mitigate loss, there will be no need to incur third party accountants costs in producing such basic information. Existing employees will be able to do it. The clause provides support from insurers where extensive further work is required over and above the calculation and submission of the claim initially.

Having required the production of information, in the absence of evidence questioning its integrity, it can be accepted without the need to audit it.

## 7.5 ACCOUNTS DESIGNATION CLAUSE

The accounts designation clause again is a clarification of the principle of indemnity. Essentially, insurers confirm that they will accept the designation and classification of costs and expenses normally used in the accounts of the insured business for policy purposes.

This can arise as an issue with regard to the definition of Purchases. This will establish the extent of uninsured costs, and consequently the adequacy of the gross profit declaration. It will also provide the relevant Rate of Gross Profit to apply to any reduction in turnover. In the case of purchases, if a declaration linked policy has been arranged, then inadvertent underinsurance is avoided though the dangers of a fundamentally low declaration remain.

The accounts designation clause, it should be noted, will not assist where the accounts are silent in respect of assets or income streams. Difficulties will not relate to the accounts designation, that will be a matter of fact. Any difficulty will relate to the adequacy of the stock sum insured if no allowance has been made for the cost involved (which will not appear on the statement of financial position)

## 7.6 ACCUMULATED STOCKS CLAUSE

The accumulated stocks clause anticipates a situation where a manufacturing business depletes its buffer stockholding to avoid a reduction in turnover and has not had an opportunity to build such buffer stock backup by the end of the Maximum Indemnity Period. If the stock has not been replaced at that point then the risk of an uninsured loss occurring presents itself. Whilst there is a common law duty to mitigate a loss generally, there is no onus on an insured business to mitigate a loss claimable under an insurance policy at the expense of incurring a loss that is not insured. The accumulated stocks clause anticipates, therefore, not only that there is a risk of loss occurring after the end of the Maximum Indemnity Period but assumes that losses are actually suffered.

In practice, many claims are settled shortly after the end of the Maximum Indemnity Period, if not before. In the majority of cases where there is a depletion of the finished stock, the business is assumed to have suffered loss in that its assets are reduced and there is a risk existent that did not exist prior to the incident, rather than requiring specific evidence of lost turnover. If a business is operating at capacity within normal hours, additional costs such as overtime working are likely to arise to recreate the stock and these are commonly held to satisfy the requirement for financial loss to be suffered.

Without the clarification of this clause, an insured business may find itself in an unpleasant position. If buffer stock was not depleted to avoid orders being lost, then a failure to mitigate might be a reasonable charge to bring. If the buffer, therefore, is reduced without there being any compensation for the subsequent recreation, then an unintended uninsured loss would arise. It should be emphasised that this clause relates to undamaged stock which is depleted for the benefit of the business interruption policy rather than damaged stock which will be dealt with under the stock cover. An accumulated stocks payment would be made under the business interruption cover as it represents a cost incurred to avoid a loss of turnover within the defined Maximum Indemnity Period.

In making this last observation it should be emphasised that the depletion of buffer stock which presents potential loss has to arise at the end of the Maximum Indemnity Period and not merely subsist at the end of the actual indemnity period if this is shorter. If additional cost is incurred in building stock backup after the claimed indemnity period but within the Maximum Indemnity Period then the additional cost of remanufacturing would be dealt with as an increased cost in the normal manner and the actual indemnity period would be extended.

Finally, there are situations where levels of buffer stock have been reduced after an incident, the business finding that the lower level of buffer remains acceptable. The occurrence of an insured incident causes management to respond to scenarios that would not normally be contemplated. Occasionally, there are strategic beneficial lessons to be gained. In the situation where buffer stock has been reduced and that has avoided a loss of turnover, if there is an intention to maintain the buffer stock at that reduced level, then it would be inappropriate to make a claim under the accumulated stocks clause.

This cover does not represent a compensatory payment relating to the stock reduction, but is rather an indemnity contribution to the cost of recreation. If there is no stock recreation, or if there is no turnover loss demonstrable after the end of the Maximum Indemnity Period directly resulting from the postponement of a turnover loss within the Maximum Indemnity Period via the use of the buffer, then no claim is appropriate.

## 7.7 DEPARTMENTAL CLAUSE

The departmental clause requires that 'if the Business is conducted in different departments, the independent trading results of which are ascertainable' then the business interruption cover will be applied in relation to that department. Typically, on a group basis, each subsidiary will represent a department. Within an individual limited company there may be distinct divisions that run independently, loss affecting one but not the other(s).

If a particular segment of business is affected by an incident, the loss will most accurately be measured by the financial information relating to that business section rather than to the business overall. If a business manufactures beverages and also maintains a unit that processes cocoa, then the average profitability of the business overall may be significantly different from the profit of a particular department.

The application of the departmental clause is not optional. The insured business cannot invoke this clause on a unilateral basis (and commonly when the section of business affected is more profitable than average).

Whilst insurers would have no difficulty in a departmental approach being taken, an insured business might be tempted to argue that the policy only allows for an average rate. Setting out an explicit departmental clause on the face of the policy is consequently for the benefit of the policyholder to clarify the fact that more meaningful detailed figures will be utilised in calculating settlement where these are available.

There are businesses that take the concept of the departmental approach to the extreme and seek to claim a specific profit for a transaction or series of transactions. The departmental clause does not provide for this. Inevitably, the section or department of a business will have an average rate of profit which reflects the mix of products sold therein. There is no policy entitlement to adopt a micro approach to the issue of calculation of the Rate of Gross Profit, though the agreement of both parties to do so would permit it.

There is no definition of what a 'department' comprises other than requiring that the segment of the business entity to which the term applies should generate independent trading results which are ascertainable. In a manufacturing business, products may pass through a variety of processes and the selling price ultimately may be built-up using charge out rates for specific machines. Notwithstanding such notional charge out rates, it would be unlikely for each machine process to be a separate profit centre within the books and records and the departmental approach, therefore, would not allow a period of downtime to be valued in terms of lost turnover by taking the number of hours lost multiplied by the notional charge out rate for the machine. There would be a need to demonstrate a turnover loss for the business segment overall.

## 7.8 SALVAGE SALE CLAUSE

The salvage sale clause relates to a situation where a business will sell stock damaged by an insured incident (whether smoke, water or impact damage) at a reduced price rather than selling it to salvage dealers. The salvage sale proceeds will invariably be significantly greater than those which a dealer would be able to offer, and the availability of discounted stock would potentially help stimulate customer interest in the business and generate turnover over and above that directly generated by the discounted goods. Customers might purchase undamaged stock (if there is any) at full price when they buy discounted salvage, although there is a danger that the opposite may happen.

The salvage sale may be a one-off event, where all stock available for sale represents salvage, or the salvage may be sold in parcels over a period of time alongside good stock. To some extent, the approach may be dictated by the extent of Damage to the Premises. If there is extensive smoke Damage throughout the building, then it might be advisable to sell-off as much of the smoke damaged stock as possible prior to refurbishment and cleaning being undertaken. Progressive discounts might be offered such that the stock is removed at a point convenient to commencement of general cleaning within the overall mitigation strategy.

The selling price (and, therefore, the Gross Profit earned) in respect of product in a salvage sale will be lower than normal. It is recognised that it is, therefore, unfair to treat it as actual turnover to be credited to the business interruption claim in the normal way. Normally, in calculating a business interruption loss, any Actual Turnover achieved is deducted from Standard Turnover and a payment is made in respect of the Reduction in Turnover at the Rate of Gross Profit from the accounts ended most recently prior to the incident. It is assumed implicitly that both the Standard Turnover and the Actual Turnover generate the same average Rate of Gross Profit. In the case of a salvage sale, such an assumption will not be valid.

To reflect this, and to avoid penalising the insured business, the actual salvage turnover is not deducted from standard turnover in calculating the reduction, though any other actual turnover outside the scope of a salvage sale would be. The Rate of Gross Profit is applied to the shortfall in turnover to calculate a loss of Gross Profit (which excludes any adjustment for or inclusion of salvage sale turnover at that point). The Gross Profit generated by the salvage sale is then deducted as a separate item from the previously calculated loss of Gross Profit to provide the loss of Gross Profit to be included in the settlement. By dealing with the salvage profit as a separate item, the insured business is not penalised for the lower level of profitability that a salvage sale will generate.

Difficulty can arise where a stock settlement is being sought in advance of a business interruption settlement. In such a situation, an insured business may make a notional contribution to retain salvage themselves (effectively submitting a blind tender alongside salvage dealers), accepting a lower settlement in respect of stock in return for the right to retain it themselves.

This can distort the subsequent profit in a salvage sale as the cost of the stock for salvage sale purposes will no longer be the historic cost price, but will be restated at the level of the deduction from the stock claim which effectively comprises the price that the insured business has paid to the insurer to retain the stock itself. A subjective assessment has to be made of the value of the affected stock. When it is sold in the salvage sale, the financial loss arising from the stock damage will crystallise via a reduced selling price. If the loss in value of stock which is actually crystallised in the salvage sale is significantly different to the assumption made when the insured business calculated the amount it would be prepared to pay to retain the salvage itself, a distortion can arise.

It is recommended that a stock settlement be left open, therefore, until a salvage sale is completed. At that point, the loss suffered is crystallised and can be apportioned between the business interruption and stock covers objectively, rather than on the basis of assumption.

Avoidable complications arise due to the fact that a depressed selling price on salvage sale is partly a material damage issue and partly a business interruption issue. An insured business may be tempted to argue that if a selling price is reduced from that which would otherwise be expected, but that nevertheless exceeds the historic cost, then the claim solely relates to business interruption rather than stock.

Whilst any material damage excess might thereby be avoided, this is nevertheless not a clever argument. If it is wholly a business interruption issue, then the material damage proviso might not be satisfied and the claim might fail in its entirety. At any rate, the reason that the selling prices have reduced, whether those ultimately achieved remained higher than cost or not, is because of the physical damage suffered. Part of the claim relates to the stock and part to the business interruption. If there is a policy cover difficulty in respect of one of those sections of the policy (stock underinsurance, for example) then the impact of an error in properly apportioning a loss between business interruption and stock could produce hardship. Making an assumption (with regards the correct level of payment to retain the salvage) to settle a stock claim unduly early is likely to bring about error.

There is no specific requirement to include a salvage sale clause on the face of the policy. The application of the clause will generally be to the benefit of the insured person and there is unlikely to be a complaint if it is introduced. That can contrast with the departmental clause which will not always be to the benefit of the insured business and in respect of which there is a greater need for explicit incorporation.

## CHAPTER 8
# CLAIMS MANAGEMENT

### 8.0 OVERVIEW OF BUSINESS INTERRUPTION CLAIM

A business interruption claim is triggered by material or physical damage to insured property caused by an insured peril e.g. fire or earthquake. This need not be the building the business operates from. It could be the plant, equipment or even just stock. In Nigeria, the material damage and the business interruption cover are usually included in one insurance policy.

Once triggered by insured property damage, the business interruption covered is the period of time the business is affected by that damage. The interruption must be due to the physical damage sustained, not by the peril insured against (i.e. the earthquake). The maximum indemnity period and a sum insured or insured gross profit would have been agreed at inception and will be shown on the policy schedule. Typically, if prevention of access cover has been bought, losses resulting from interruption as a consequence of damage to property in the vicinity of the insured business, preventing or hindering the use of or access to the business will be covered up to a stated limit. There are also a number of extensions which broadens the definition of the product and have now grown into a separate product in some jurisdictions (Supply Chain Risk/Contingent Business Interruption – where material damage may no longer be required to trigger a claim.)

There are two key elements to business interruption cover. The first is loss of gross profit, designed to cover loss of business income and any on-going costs that the company has to cover even when not trading for example, paying key staff. The other is increased cost of working, which recognises that after an unexpected event, the company needs to spend extra money to keep the business going as best as possible, perhaps by renting alternative premises, hiring additional staff or arranging for additional advertising to let customers know when they are back in business. To benefit from this aspect of cover, though, the company must show how any spending claimed for is cost-effective in reducing the potential loss of business income. This is often referred to as the economic limit test.

While the concept itself is relatively straightforward, Business Interruption insurance claims can be very tricky. Issues common to many Business Interruption insurance claims include:

- Has there been damage to trigger the cover?
- Did the Business Interruption losses arise from that damage?
- How should the Business Interruption losses be calculated?

## 8.1. LEGAL AND OTHER ISSUES TO CONSIDER FOR CLAIMS PRESENTATION:

Sometimes disputes arise when presenting business interruption claims to insurers. Some of these issues bother on law, interpretation of contract, judicial precedence, customs and practice. Whilst there are virtually no judicial cases in Nigeria on this subject, sometimes arguments have been made using cases from UK, Europe and America in the course of claims presentation and adjustments. A few of such issues will be examined here.

### 8.1.1 What Principles of Law should be considered

There are several principles of insurance law that favour policyholders which should serve as the foundation for any legal analysis and/or presentation of a particular business interruption

claim. Because such principles favour policyholders, insurers often do not advise the insureds of the benefits of applying such principles to the claim at stake. Thus, it is incumbent upon the insured and broker to understand such principles and make sure that are applied to the claim to maximise coverage.

Choice of Law. The Insurance Act 2003 is the principal legal document for insurance practice in Nigeria. The wordings of the policy document (contract) is equally important and is expected to be interpreted based on the rules of interpretation at common law and in line with Nigerian practice. This is one of the more perplexing principles to keep in mind when analysing an insurance coverage issue. The importance of this issue cannot be overstated, because insurers often ignore this principle when they rely on case laws outside the Nigerian jurisdiction to support their declinations of coverage. As persuasive as it may be, a decided case in other jurisdiction is not sufficient to form the basis of repudiating a Nigerian claim. Insurers will do well to test matters in Nigerian courts in order to establish precedents. Thus, whenever the policyholder receives a declination letter from its insurer, the policyholder /broker really must analyse the insurer's position under the law. The important point to remember when it comes to choice of law issues for adjusting business interruption claims is that the insurer may be relying on law that will not, or likely will not, be applied to the policy at stake.

### 8.1.2 Practical Construction

Insurers often ignore a little-known principle of insurance contract interpretation known as the doctrine of "practical construction". That doctrine provides that parties to a contract, by their conduct, can give meaning to the contract. The rule of practical construction is predicated on the common sense concept that "actions speak louder than words". When the parties to a contract perform under a contract and demonstrate by their conduct that they knew what they were talking about, the courts should enforce that intent. One question a broker or loss assessor should always ask a client when advising on an insurance claim is whether the client and its insurer have previously adjusted a similar loss on either the same policy or prior policy containing the same or similar wordings than the current policy. If so, it should be determined whether the insurer's past conduct can be used to the policyholder's advantage for the claim at stake. For example, did the insurer provide coverage on the prior claim? Did the insurer take a position on the prior claim that favours coverage for the policyholder on the current claim?

### 8.1.3 Insurer's Conduct On Other Insureds' Claims

An insurer often overlooks the rule of insurance contract construction that its own conduct in connection with claims by other insureds can give meaning to its policy for another policyholder. If an insurer takes a particular position with respect to the client's claim that is contrary to a position that the insurer has taken on a similar claim by another client, such conduct can be used to argue that the wording/language should be interpreted in favour of the client. Courts have allowed discovery of such "other insured" information for several reasons. Some courts reason that information showing the insurer's understanding of its own policy language can be used to provide meaning to the language, because one rule of construing ambiguous policy language is that the insurer's understanding of what the insured thought the language meant, or could think the language meant, may be applied. Other courts reason that "other insured" information is relevant because it can be used to support the policyholder's argument that the policy language is ambiguous and that the policyholder's proffered interpretation of the policy language is reasonable. It is interesting to note that some of the law on this issue has come from disputes between insurers and their reinsurers.

### 8.1.4 Is A Complete Cessation Of Operations Needed To Trigger Business Interruption Claim

One of the contested business interruption coverage issues in recent years is the position being taken by certain insurers in some jurisdictions outside Nigeria that a complete cessation of all activities at the insured's location must occur in order for business interruption coverage to be triggered. In other words, according to such insurers, a covered peril that merely impairs operations or only causes part of the operations to cease does not give rise to covered business interruption coverage. This of course will sound ridiculous to any client. How does this position work?

Assume that the insured has a factory housing 10 machines producing sugar and a covered peril destroys five of the machines, but the other five continue to produce sugar. According to certain insurers, there is no business interruption coverage because operations were only "impaired", they were not "interrupted". Any broker representing a client faced with this position should vigorously resist it; it goes against all reasonable expectations of the insured and the explanation of business interruption coverage proffered by many insurers when explaining such coverage during policy placement. The significant issues relates to lost turnover, increase in cost of working, etc. Once that is established, business interruption claim should be triggered.

### 8.1.5 Can The Insured Location Be Divided Into Separate Operating Units

Assume that the client's premises are a shopping mall with cinema, supermarkets, clubhouse and a hotel. What if only a portion of the operations sustains physical loss or damage. Say one of the supermarkets, two out of 10 cinema halls, or three out of 12 floors at the hotel were affected by fire. The reality is that the income of the entire premises is adversely affected. Under such circumstances, insurers often argue that the client is entitled to business interruption coverage only for that particular portion of the property that sustained physical loss or damage. The insurer's position on this issue should be challenged. Courts have long recognised that a premises insured under a business interruption policy may have several parts to it, and that physical loss to one part of the premises may cause a business interruption loss for the entire premises. The reasoning applied by such courts applies equally to an insured premise that has several component parts.

### 8.1.6 Must The Policyholder Demonstrate That It Lost Turnover/Sales

Sometimes a policy is not clear on what quantum of proof an insured must present to show a business interruption loss. In such circumstances, insurers sometimes argue that the insured did not suffer any business interruption loss because the insured could not prove that it actually lost turnover or sales. Indeed, many courts recognise business interruption coverage for policyholders who merely show lost production. Sometimes, neither the court nor the policy clearly addresses the difference between a loss of production and a loss of turnover. Well-structured policies would expressly provide that the loss can be valued on a loss of production basis where the turnover basis is unable to demonstrate the loss.

### 8.1.7 What If The Policyholder Sustains An Interdependent Business Interruption Loss

The term "interdependency" is often referred to in business interruption parlance to denote that a particular operation of the insured is dependent upon certain other operations of the insured in order to produce income because the other operations act as either providers of raw materials or consumers of products or services. Imagine a beverage producing company that also maintains a cocoa plantation and production facility. Must an insured's policy expressly state that it provides "interdependent" business interruption coverage in order for a policyholder to be entitled to such coverage? Some courts have not required such express wording but rather reason that such coverage would be expected by the insured. This underscores the importance of describing the business of the insured as stated in previous chapters. The issue of "interdependent" and "contingent" business interruption coverage is best addressed during policy placement and/or renewal with express policy wording/language. However, if such issues were not expressly addressed, the policy language that was used should be carefully examined at claims time to determine how the policyholder can maximise coverage for the claim it is presenting to its insurer.

### 8.1.8 The Future Of Business Interruption Coverage Disputes – Cyber related Losses

Businesses are increasingly reliant on computers, internet, robotics, artificial intelligence, etc. Never before has a company had so many ways to provide expansive, immediate access to a tremendous amount of up-to-date information to the company's employees, customers and suppliers with Internet home pages, intranets, networks, etc. Increased efficiency and profits are sure to be realised. But just as sure, such increasing reliance on computers, coupled with the increased access by so many persons to information on those computers and elsewhere, exposes companies to new areas of risks. What happens when a computer virus accidentally or intentionally is introduced into any of the company's computer-related platforms, whether it is its home page on the World Wide Web or its intranet or network, and eventually wipes out vital computer data or otherwise corrupts all or part of the company's computer network. Is such a loss covered by traditional business interruption insurance? What happens when an employee steals important computer data because of the new access given to employees via the company's intranet? What if the employee steals or corrupts such data not for his/her personal gain but just to cause loss to the company? What if the person responsible for such theft or corruption of data is not an employee of the company but rather some other person, such as a computer hacker? Are these types of losses covered by business interruption insurance?

These questions and others are causing many in the insurance profession to take a fresh look at how traditional insurance policies would respond to such losses. Where there are potential problems, some policyholders are seeking enhancements to coverage. Some insurers already are responding to this new reality of insuring cyber related losses. Generally, Cyber Liability policies provides a first and third party protection. Part of the first party coverage is a Business Interruption coverage following a cyber attack. Policies are beginning to emerge where the cyber risks is extended on the regular business interruption policy.

**8.1.9 Loss Of Computer Data - Does It Trigger Business Inter-**

## ruption Coverage

One of the first issues that is being asked when analysing coverage for computer related losses is whether loss to computer data alone without loss or damage to the CPU or any other property involves "direct physical loss or damage" to property sufficient to trigger business interruption coverage. Some coverage experts, especially within insurance companies, say "no" because computer data is not tangible property therefore, such data cannot itself sustain "direct physical loss or damage". Such persons say that loss of intangible property such as computer data is not sufficient to trigger business interruption coverage. Other coverage experts disagree. They argue that computer data is, indeed, tangible property, so that the loss thereof or loss of use thereof triggers business interruption coverage. Some argue that, even if computer data itself is not tangible property, loss caused by computer viruses and the like in reality involve physical injury to the hard drive of a computer and that that loss is direct physical loss to tangible property. Given this debate, it behoves all policyholders to address computer data loss issues in the policy placement process rather than wait to "fight it out" during claims. Cyber policies or Cyber extensions remains with the best way out given that business interruption is an integral part of the Cyber Liability coverage. Insurers should also be explicit in their wordings if the intension is not to provide coverage.

### 8.2.0 STEPS TO TAKE IMMEDIATELY FOLLOWING A LOSS

The following guide will assist the claimant or persons handling insurance within the affected organization.

1. Report the claim to your broker/agent or your insurance company.
2. Restore fire protection.
3. Take immediate action to minimize the loss.
4. Protect undamaged property from loss.
5. Implement means of capturing all expenses.
6. Consult contractors for an initial estimate of the scope

and cost of repairs.
7. Define plans as to reopening the location and under what conditions.
8. Identify temporary measures needed to resume operations and the associated extraordinary
9. expenses that are incurred.
10. Take photographs of the damage.
11. Appoint one person to represent your company with the adjuster.
12. Set up clear lines of communication with the adjuster and ensure that all personnel understand the functions of the adjuster, experts, brokers, etc.

Assign one special work order code to the loss to which all costs can be charged. Specific items should be grouped into one of the following categories with as many sub accounts as needed:

1. Cleanup
2. Debris Removal
3. Protection and Preservation of Property
4. Buildings and Structures
5. Machinery and Equipment
6. Furniture, Fixtures and Supplies
7. Property of Customers and Employees
8. Excess Operating Costs:
   a. to mitigate earnings losses
   b. to operate as normally as possible

Descriptions of work performed, services purchased or materials consumed help the insurance adjuster visualize and evaluate the claim. Two types of descriptions are needed: general descriptions of work orders or cost centers used to gather claimable costs, and specific descriptions of individual costs being claimed. Work order descriptions contained in authorization materials or periodic summaries are usually adequate. Descriptions of in-house labour charges may have to be prepared separately by supervisors or department heads. If so, a system should be developed early to provide the necessary detail. Descriptions of contractor charges and supplier invoices can usually be obtained from purchasing documentation.

A sequence of events leading up to the loss and following the loss should be prepared as soon as practical. The events sequence should include:

1. Description of the incident
2. Cause of incident (if known)
3. Events leading up to incident (with dates and times)
4. Description of impact on the property and operations
5. Description of what will be done to minimize the loss

It is necessary to accumulate operating data to calculate the business interruption loss and to prepare for audit of the claim. You should be prepared to address the following:

1. What is the production capacity of the plant, line or machine that was
2. damaged?
3. At what percentage were you operating at the time of the loss?
4. At what rate did you expect to produce during the "loss period"?
5. "Loss Period" is the period from when the damage prevents the asset from producing until that asset is up and running at the same rate and quality as it was just prior to the loss.
6. How many shifts per day do you operate?
7. How many shifts per day, week or month do you dedicate to maintenance?
8. Will all product lines be affected, or just some?
9. Will you be able to supply customers from inventory during the loss period?
10. Are you able to access other production facilities in your system to produce for you while you are down?
11. If you have other facilities produce for you, are their

costs higher or lower than yours?
12. How much production was/will be lost during the down time?
13. How much production can be made up with overtime and how long will it take you to make it up?
14. If you have to draw down on inventory to meet orders, how long will it take you to replenish inventories to the quantities you enjoyed before the loss?
15. At what point does depletion of your inventories become critical?

After you have answered the above, you can begin quantifying the loss. To do so, you will have to provide the following information:

1. Production records, inventory records, cost summary data records and turnover/income statements for 3-6-12 months prior to the loss. The cost summary data sheets should show in the minutest detail the elements of the variable and fixed costs.
2. Detail breakdown of your hourly payroll fringes and the percentage of fringe to hourly payroll?
3. Was there any express freight/transport to get product to customers in excess of normal?
4. Did you have to rent any assets while your damaged assets were being repaired or replaced?
5. Indicate the peaks and valleys of your production and sales year.
6. If you cannot transfer production from the site of loss to another site, explain why.
7. Do you have any agreements with your employees, their bargaining agencies (union) or outside vendors that compel you to pay employees though no work is available?
8. Did you have plant turnaround schedule during the period that now falls within the loss period? Can that turnaround be rescheduled? Will you reschedule?

Most business interruption loss calculations take the form of projections of what would have occurred had no loss happened. Projections are generally based on actual operations prior to a loss and expected operations had no loss occurred. For example, a simple projection of lost production might take the form of:

| | |
|---|---|
| Production 3 months prior to loss | 1,250,320 diapers |
| Operating days | 90 days |
| Projected production per day | 13,740 diapers |
| Days interrupted | 10 days |
| Lost production | 137,400 diapers |

Similar base period type calculations will be necessary to determine net sales/turnover values of the lost production, variable (saved) manufacturing costs, and production makeup. Each factor in a calculation needs to be documented. Additional historical data needs to be supplied to allow insurance company representatives or adjuster to test the reasonableness of the various calculations. While documenting your production loss is the first step, your insurer will ultimately need to be convinced that you lost turnover/sales. They will look at historical production, inventory levels, and sales.

It is necessary to accumulate operating and other data to document the business interruption loss and to prepare for the audit of the claim. Data, in the form of reports, may include:

1. Prior income/turnover records
2. Prior income statement
3. Trend reports and projections
4. External factors impacting operations

The time period to be used may vary depending upon many factors. Those factors may include the type of operations impacted, the historical stability of those operations, external impacts not readily ascertainable from historical data alone, and the period of interruption in question. Determinations are best made with proper accounting methods. Your broker will work with your accounting staff, or outside accountants, in determining the appropriate basis to be used to ensure proper measurement of loss.

The projection of lost turnover/revenues may be addressed by various methods. The time of year, type of product/service, period of interruption, economic conditions, competition and various other factors must be considered. Typically, historical data will form the basis and that data is then trended to project the turnover that would have been made had no loss occurred. For an earnings claim, the presentation might ultimately result in the following form with detailed support:

| | |
|---|---|
| Lost Turnover/Revenue | 100,000 |
| Less: Cost of Sales | 55,000 |
| Gross Earnings | 45,000 |
| Less: Uninsurred Operating Expenses | 20,000 |
| Earnings Loss | 25,000 |

The above is similar to applying a rate of gross profit (25% in this instance) to the lost turnover.

Excess operating costs (increase in cost of workings) that are incurred as a direct result of physical damage to insured property may be recoverable in the claim. These costs generally fit one of two categories: 1) Costs to mitigate or reduce an earnings loss; and 2) Costs to operate as normally as possible while the business is being restored without minimizing loss. These are extra, or extraordinary expenses. Documentation of costs and purpose is required. Good documentary support is essential for these items. Examples of excess operating costs (increase in cost of workings) are as follows:

1. Expediting expenses on repair projects
2. Temporary facility use to minimize loss
3. The excess cost of services/products obtained from

competitors in order to serve your customers
4. Equipment rental
5. Security service during repairs
6. Expenses incurred to operate using other resources to meet requirement of customer contracts
7. Extra Labour
8. Overtime

The final claim presentation represents the culmination of many hours of hard work, strategy and negotiation. Differences of opinion between you and the adjuster may occur, and all claims are not covered. The role of your broker is to facilitate the adjustment process and ensure that you receive every benefit afforded by your insurance program. Yours is to ensure that your costs are properly documented and presented for discussions.

# CHAPTER 9
# CLAIMS MANAGEMENT – WORKED EXAMPLES

## 9.1. Example 1

Ekomeme Manufacturing Plc, a company located at Agege, Lagos produces cereals for children below 10 years. The company's premises was damaged by fire on 1st January, 2019. At the time, the company had business interruption cover in force as follows:

Gross Profit          900,000.00

Maximum Indemnity Period:          12 months

Immediately after the fire, repairs on building were put in place and new machinery ordered. It was estimated that the business would return to full production on 31st March, 2019 but due to a flood incident at one of the suppliers' premises, full production was not resumed until 1st May, 2019. The company regained its market share on 1st August 2019

The company sub-contracted work out to Temi Ventures, a friendly rival at a cost of 115,000.00 to avoid a further reduction in turnover of 294,000.00. As a result of the above, savings were made in overtime wages of 20,000.00 and in fixed expenses of 50,000.00.

Prior to the loss, turnover had been growing at a steady rate of 15% per annum with the rate of gross profit maintained at the previous year's level. The insured's audited accounts for the year ended 31st December 2018 showed the following figures:

| | |
|---|---|
| Standard Turnover: | 860,000.00 |
| Actual Turnover: | 384,000.00 |
| Turnover | 2,500,000.00 |
| Work in progress as at 31/12/18 | 50,000.00 |
| Stock as at 31/12/18 | 200,000.00 |
| Work in progress as at 1/1/18 | 60,000.00 |
| Stock as at 1/1/18 | 190,000.00 |
| Purchases | 1,400,000.00 |
| Carriages | 10,000.00 |

| | |
|---|---|
| Diesel & Power | 40,000.00 |
| Commission | 50,000.00 |
| Salaries | 350,000.00 |
| Fixed expenses | 550,000.00 |
| Net Profit | 100,000.00 |

From the information provided, what would be the loss payable under the business interruption policy?

### Suggested Solution to Example 1

The key components of the loss revolves around lost gross profit and increase in cost of working. Given the information provided, we can calculate the gross profit (insurance definition) and determine its rate as well. The difference basis of gross profit computation will be used. The turnover during the indemnity period (actual turnover) will be compared with the standard turnover to determine if a reduction has occurred. Any reduction will be multiplied by the rate of gross profit to determine the lost gross profit. A similar approach would have been used had they been wages.

**Gross Profit:** {Turnover + Closing Stock + Work in Progress (closing)} −{Opening Stock + Work in Progress (opening) + Specified Working Expenses}

Gross Profit = (2,500,000 + 200,000 + 50,000) − (190,000 + 60,000 + 1,400,000 + 10,000 + 40,000 + 50,000)

= 2,750,000 − 1,750,000

Gross Profit = 1,000,000

**Rate of Gross Profit:** Gross Profit/turnover x 100

= 1,000,000 / 2,500,000 x 100

Rate of Gross Profit = 40%

### Reduction in Turnover

We were told that turnover grew steadily at 15% per annum. This is a business circumstance that must be considered in determining the reduction in turnover and ultimately, the lost gross profit. Thus the standard turnover of 860,000 will be marked up by 15% as follows:

$$860,000 + 15\% = 989,000$$

This adjusted standard turnover will be compared with the turnover during the indemnity period (actual turnover) of 384,000. Thus reduction will be as follows:

Adjusted Standard Turnover – Actual Turnover

$$= 989,000 - 384,000$$
$$= 605,000$$

The Lost Gross Profit out of the turnover will be derived by multiplying it with the rate of gross profit calculated above thus:

Lost Gross Profit = 605,000 x 40%

i) **Lost Gross Profit** = 242,200

Alternatively, the above could have been computed as follows:

Rate of Gross Profit (Adjusted Standard Turnover – Actual Turnover)

40% (860,000 + 15% - 384,000)

40% (989,000 - 384,000)

40% (605,000)

= 242,000

ii) **Increase in cost of working** = ₦115,000

As noted in previous chapters, Increase in Cost of Working is always subjected to the economic limit test. This is calculated as Rate of Gross Profit x Turnover achieved by incurring such cost. In this instance, 115,000 was incurred to achieve a turnover of 294,000 and will be tested as follows:

Rate of Gross Profit x Turnover Achieved

= 40% x 294,000

= 117,600

As we can see, 115,000 incurred is less than 117,600 which the economic test has revealed. This means that the increase in cost of working of 115,000 is justified and would be allowed in full for the claim.

| Savings: | Overtime | = | 20,000 |
|---|---|---|---|
| | Fixed Expenses | = | 50,000 |

**Compilation of Claim:**

| i) | Lost Gross Profit | = | 242,000 |
|---|---|---|---|
| ii) | Plus increase in cost of working | = | 115,000 |
| | | | 357,000 |
| | Less Savings | | 70,000 |
| **Loss** | | | **287,000** |

**Check for Adequacy of sum Insured and Average:**

Rate of Gross Profit x Annual Turnover + Growth Rate

= 40% (2,500,000 + 15%)

= 40% (2,875,000)

= 1,150,000

The above shows that Ekomeme Manufacturing Plc should have insured its gross profit for 1,150,000. Unfortunately, the company underinsured for 900,000 and must therefore bear the consequences.

## Claim Payable

Since the sum insured of 900,000 is less than 1,150,000, the insurer will apply average as follows:

Sum Insured/Value at     x     loss

900,000 / 1,150,000     x     287,000

= **224,608.70**

## 9.2 Example 2

Wumpet Limited manufactures ladies bags in Surulere, Lagos.

Due to the company's previous experience, a declaration linked business interruption policy was recently put in place. The company's estimated gross profit for the 2020 year of Insurance is 1,470,000.

The following figures were forwarded to Benefits Loss Adjusters in support of the claim:

| | |
|---|---|
| Turnover in 2019 (previous financial year) - | 3,360,000 |
| Gross Profit in 2019 - | 1,470,000 |
| Standard Turnover - | 1,050,000 |
| Turnover during the Indemnity Period - | 420,000 |
| Increase in cost of working that prevented a loss of Turnover of (105,000) - | 63,000 |
| Savings - | 78,750 |

Benefit Loss Adjusters agreed with an upward trend of 21% in view of the fact that the competitor has gone out of business. Calculate the loss payable.

### Suggested Solution to Example 2

The components of loss are the same as example 1 above in terms of lost gross profit and increase in cost of workings. The explanation provided above will suffice in most cases.

**Rate of Gross Profit** = Gross Profit/Turnover x 100

= 1,470,000 / 3,360,000 x 100

= 43.75%

(i) **Lost Gross Profit** =

Rate of Gross Profit (Standard Turnover – Turnover during the Indemnity Period)

43.75% (1,050,000 +21% - 420,000)

43.75% (1,270,500 – 420,000)

43.75% (850,500)

372,093.75

(ii) **Increase in cost of working** = 63,000

Economic Limit = Rate of Gross Profit x Turnover achieved

= 105,000 x 43.75%

= **45,937.50**

In this instance, the economic limit test shows that 63,000 was not reasonable or justifiable as it is higher than the economic limit of 45,937.50. The loss adjuster will therefore limit the loss to 45,937.50.

**Compilation of Claim:**

| | |
|---|---|
| Loss of Gross Profit | 372,093.75 |
| Increase in Cost of Working | 45,937.50 |
| | 418,031.25 |
| Less Savings | 78,750.00 |
| **Loss** | **339,281.25** |

As the policy is declaration linked, average will not apply. It is therefore not necessary to check for the adequacy of sums insured. The insurer will pay 339,281.25.

## 9.3 Example 3

Nene & Ranti Limited operates an event centre at Iju Ishaga area of Ogun State. Its building and facilities were severely damaged as a result of impact from an ill-fated aircraft in 2013. Due to the damage and regulatory investigations into the plane crash, the business was interrupted for 4 months. The account manager has presented you with the following details in respect of their business interruption insurance claims:

| | | |
|---|---|---|
| Gross Profit Sum Insurance | - | 1,000,000 |
| Indemnity Period | - | 12 months |
| Turnover during interruption Period | - | 1,500,000 |

Turnover during corresponding period in 2012 - 3,750,000
Increase in cost of working - 250,000
Which avoided a further reduction in turnover of - 750,000
Gross Profit in 2012 (the last financial year) - 1,500,000
Turnover in 2012 - 6,000,000
Turnover which would have been achieved in twelve (12) months from the date of damage - 7,800,000
Savings - 50,000

Determine the claim payable.

## Suggested Solution to Example 3

Example 3 is similar to example 1 in many respects. We will therefore adopt the same processes of determining the rate of gross profit, reduction in turnover, lost gross profit, increase in cost of working as well as checking for the adequacy of the sum insured.

### Rate of Gross Profit

Gross Profit in the previous year / Turnover in the previous year x 100

= 1,500,000 / 6,000,000

=    25%

Reduction in Turnover = Standard Turnover - Turnover during indemnity period

= 3,750,000 – 1,500,000

= 2,250,000

   i)   Lost Gross Profit = Rate of Gross Profit x Reduction in Turnover

25% x 2,250,000 = 562,500

   ii)   Increase in cost of working

Check for economic limit which is the maximum cost recoverable.

Turnover saved x Rate of Gross Profit = 750,000 x 25%

= 187,500

Although 250,000, the policy will only pay 187,500

## Compilation of Claim

| | | |
|---|---|---|
| Loss of Gross Profit | = | 562,500 |
| Increase in Cost of Working | = | 187,500 |
| | = | 750,000 |
| Less Savings | = | 50,000 |
| Loss | = | 700,000 |

## Check for Adequacy of sum Insured and Average:

Rate of Gross Profit x Annual Turnover + Growth Rate

In the example, we were told that turnover which would have been achieved in 12 months is 7,800,000. This means the growth rate of turnover is 30%. We will go ahead and use the figure given and multiply same with the rate of gross profit as follows:

= 7,800,000 x 25%

= 1,950,000

The above shows that Nene & Ranti Limited should have insured its gross profit for 1,950,000. Unfortunately, the company underinsured for 1,000,000 and must therefore bear the consequences.

Claim Payable

Since the sum insured of 1,000,000 is less than 1,950,000, the insurer will apply average as follows:

Sum Insured/Value at      x     loss

1,000,000 / 1,950,000     x     700,000

Claim   =   358,974.36

## 9.4. Important Note

Sometimes the turnover due to certain distortions might not prove a loss. For instance, the price of goods or services may have been increased shortly before the interruption. A direct comparison between the standard turnover and turnover during the indemnity period might not reveal a loss. In such circumstances, it might be expedient to make use of production/manufactured unit. The example below buttresses this point:

| Bassey Enterprise | | |
|---|---|---|
| Determination of Claims | | |
| | Turnover | Manufactured units |
| Standard Period | 422,382,075.33 | 924,061,121.49 |
| Indemnity Period | 565,340,568.30 | 845,897,038.90 |
| Reduction/(Excess) in Turnover | (142,958,492.97) | 78,164,082.59 |
| Gross Profit Rate | 22.48% | 22.48% |
| Claim (Gross Profit) | FALSE | 17,571,286.00 |
| Increase cost of working | | 4,610,400.00 |
| Wages Rate | | 7% |
| Wages Claim | | 5,471,485.78 |
| Total Claims | | 27,653,171.78 |

## 9.5. Practice Question

The following information was extracted from the books of FASCON Limited.

Sum Insured on Dual Payroll – 45 million

Maximum Indemnity Period - 24 Months

Cover – 13 Weeks Initial Period 40% Remainder

Alternative Period – 49 weeks.

**Information about interruption following a flood damage which occurred on 1ˢᵗ July, 2019 include:**

Indemnity Period – 1ˢᵗ July to 30ᵗʰ November, 2019

Shortage in Turnover for the 1ˢᵗ 13 weeks – 65million Remainder Period – 24million

Savings in payroll during Initial Period – 1.2million

Annual Turnover – 460million.

Payroll in 2018 – 40million 2018 Turnover – 160million

2.3milllion was spent to generate a turnover of 15million.

Adjust the loss

## CHAPTER 10  EMERGING ISSUES
## 10.0 GENERAL OVERVIEW:

In recent years, conversations around business interruption insurance have evolved from direct business interruption to areas such as interdependencies (loss of profit or production capacity at one corporate facility due to an adverse event at another corporate facility supplying or being supplied); contingent business interruption (loss of profit at a facility due to loss of raw materials or components from key suppliers or loss of major customers); non-damage business interruption (loss caused by incident unrelated to property damage such as pandemic, strikes, insolvency, etc.). Whilst Supply Chain business interruption is breaking away or evolving into a brand new product, Business Interruption following Cyber event is being covered under the first party section of the Cyber Liability policy.

The growing reliance on technology and data from business is beginning to manifest in business interruption and contingent business interruption claims. Companies can suffer major business interruption losses due to the unavailability of critical data or technology, either through a technical glitch, cyber-attack or a physical event, such as fire or flood. The inability to access data for an extended period of time can have a significant impact on revenues.

Dependency on digital supply chains both for the delivery of services and the supply of goods brings numerous benefits. Shared technology based platforms and blockchain enables data to be exchanged between parties, automates administrative tasks and orders and transports products on demand. Digital supply chains are more transparent and goods can be tracked back to their source. However, such platforms can potentially create a chain reaction ensuring a loss cascades through a whole sector. If a platform is unavailable due to a technical glitch or cyber event, it could bring large business interruption losses for multiple companies that all rely and share the same system. In June 2019, an outage caused a catastrophic failure at some Google cloud services, causing several hours of disruption to a number of large online service providers, including You Tube, Uber and Snapchat.

## 10.1 NON DAMAGE BUSINESS INTERRUPTION:

Non-physical damage business interruption (NDBI) has been seen as the next in the evolution of covers by some. This is because traditional business interruption insurance is no longer enough, and companies increasingly need to add to it with evolving NDBI cover. New types of solutions are providing protection against a wider range of perils, and extending insurance cover from tangible to intangible assets. Non-damage business interruption policies are designed to protect earnings even when there is no physical damage. For example, events that could trigger non damage business interruption include electricity blackouts, strikes, or cyber-attacks. Companies are covered for everything from profit losses to extra expenses incurred ensuring business continuity to contractual penalties. It is important to stress that some major global companies today own little or no assets. For companies like Airbnb (which does not own rental units) and Uber (which does not own cars), physical damage is much less of a risk priority than risks related to income streams and cash flows.

Non damage business interruption covers can either be standalone or added to an existing business interruption. The client needs to have a thorough understanding of key risks impacting cash flows and which exposures can impact revenues. Once the risks have been identified, clients need to decide if these risks are insurable with traditional insurance and what the potential impact or magnitude is.

## 10.2 CONTINGENT BUSINESS INTERRUPTION AND SUPPLY CHAIN:

In today's global marketplace, more and more businesses rely on overseas suppliers. If your company's operations depend on the timely delivery of raw materials, parts or finished products from distant locations, then your business could be hurt when these goods are delayed or fail to arrive altogether. Significant downturn in supply often results in increased costs for acquisition of the materials needed to continue operating. It can also result in partial or complete shutdown of facilities lacking the resources to operate.

Organisations can take steps to limit the impact of supply chain disruption, such as warehousing inventory and using multiple suppliers when possible. Purchasing specialty insurance policies, including contingent business interruption (CBI) insurance and supply chain insurance can also limit exposure to loss. These types of insurance reimburse businesses for lost profits and related costs caused by disruptions in supply chain even if the company itself has not suffered any damage. Significant supply chain disruptions can reduce revenue, cut into market share, threaten production and distribution, inflate costs and ultimately affect a company's bottom line. Whether you run a global company or a small business, you need the proper insurance coverage to protect against supply chain failure.

Contingent business interruption, or CBI, coverage can provide an important line of defense against losses caused by disruptions at the locations of suppliers or customers. This type of insurance is limited because it only provides coverage if the businesses you depend on are disrupted by physical property damage. For instance, if a supplier's factory is damaged by fire and ceases operations. CBI does not protect for all perils; nor does it protect a business when roads are closed and employees cannot get to work or when products cannot be distributed or other suppliers are affected.

Supply Chain Insurance provides far broader coverage than CBI insurance for business interruption caused by disruptions to the company's supply chain. In addition to covering disruptions caused by property damage to suppliers or customers' businesses, supply chain insurance can cover losses caused by a wide range of events, including:

1. Natural disasters.
2. Industrial accidents.
3. Labor issues (strikes, shortages, etc.).
4. Production process problems.
5. Political upheaval, war, civil strife.
6. Riots or other disruptive civic action.
7. Closure of roads, bridges, or other transportation infrastructure.
8. Public health emergencies; e.g., pandemics requiring quarantine like the COVID19.
9. Regulatory action.
10. Financial issues; e.g., solvency, cash flow problems.

Insurance is a critical component of managing supply chain risk, but it should not be seen as a first line of defense. Your business can also limit its exposure to supply chain risk by taking the following actions:

1. Assess your supply chain and identify risks and weaknesses.
2. Balance supply chain logistics (e.g., just-in-time delivery) with risk management.
3. Identify back-up suppliers and vendors.
4. Establish contingency plans and include supply chain disruption in your business continuity plan.

By taking these steps, business owners can make informed decisions about mitigation planning, risk transfer and levels of self-insurance. The broker can also be a valuable resource in helping the business identify risks and secure adequate insurance coverage.

Ultimately, the future will come thick and fast. The Nigerian market must act fast in the areas of policy review, new wordings and new perspectives.

## CHAPTER 11
## PANDEMICS (CORONAVIRUS) AND BUSINESS INTERRUPTION

### 8.0 GENERAL OVERVIEW

At the time of writing this book, the world is still dealing with the health and economic emergencies of COVID-19 (Coronavirus). The disease has come with great human and economic loss. As the scientific community continues to make in route into finding a vaccine, the economic pressures of total lockdown have forced countries and states to make tough decisions on easing the lockdown and returning gradually to a "normal" life.

Businesses outside of those designated as essential services were fully interrupted in some places for at least two months. Even with the gradual return to normalcy, businesses are not yet expected to return to full-staff capacity as a result of social/physical distancing. As a result, organisations have sought clarity as to whether their business interruption policies engage in this instance.

The issue of coverage will always be resolved through the interpretation of the specific policy wordings. The court will certainly be the final arbiter on this matter. Interestingly, the FCA in the UK has approached the court for interpretation to provide clarity to insurers concerning SMEs. A French court recently mandated Axa Insurance to pay a restaurant for losses sustained due to its closure as a result of COVID-19. The court predicated this on the non-damage wordings provided in the policy thus closure by government triggered the policy. Axa Insurance has challenged the ruling and the outcome is being awaited. As at date, no one has approached the court in Nigeria. The challenge in Nigeria might be that few clients pre-COVID-19 had business interruption insurance in place. There is also the issue of wordings which may not in most instances have covered non-damage perils or notifiable disease. There is also the general apathy in approaching the court on insurance matters in Nigeria.

Whatever the case might be and however the court will determine this issue, one thing is clear. The future of business interruption insurance will never be the same again in Nigeria. More clients will demand coverage including pandemics. The market will have to respond in very clear terms. Clarity regarding the level of coverage granted and the associated cost. The market will have to be specific with wordings either as an extension or new product. As noted in earlier chapters, new policies such as Contingent Business Interruption and Supply Chain is usually very clear on the coverage for pandemics.

## 8.1 COVER TRIGGERS

Without prejudice to the decision of the courts regarding business interruption coverage for Covid-19, there are a few triggers that require mentioning and examining as follows:

1) **Damage at the Premises**: As we all know, damage involves a change in the state of a thing which often requires some sort of remediation. Premises or vicinity is often well defined. In a claim situation, there will be a need to prove that damage occurred at a premises. There might be practical issues in proving that Covid-19 constitutes damage at a premises. Most operative clauses of business interruption policies in Nigeria hinges on physical damage to buildings, machines, etc. Except where non-damage wordings exist, this might be the first hurdle.

2) **Notifiable Disease**: This clause or extension is also lacking in most Nigerian policy documents. Perhaps limited experience with notifiable diseases may have been responsible for this. What is critical is the interruption following a notifiable disease and not merely the occurrence of a notifiable disease. There is also the part of insurers providing

cover for diseases transmitted from human to human with very specific exclusions such as HIV and others. Thus SARS and its strains which seems to be transmitted from animals to humans are often excluded from the notifiable disease extension. Covid-19 is now notifiable throughout Nigeria. In places where this coverage is provided, there are often presented in two variants. Some policies typically list diseases that it considers 'notifiable' for contract certainty. No one would have had the crystal ball to list Covid-19 being a novel virus. Other policies typically cover loss from diseases that are notifiable at the time of claim. Such an approach would have picked up Covid-19. However, the covered disease is commonly at the Premises or in the vicinity. Claimed business interruption loss must be caused by the occurrence. The challenge with Covid-19 is the inability of science at the moment to test the disease outside a host thus difficult to establish its presence on premises or the damaged caused to the premises. It is said that the disease does not last on a surface for a long time. This will present a practical problem in claim adjustment as evidence may never be obtained.

3) **Denial of Access/Loss of Attraction:** Most policies in Nigeria provides cover for denial of access following damage. The issue of damage as explained earlier becomes a problem when it comes to Covid-19. Thus, although access to business premises have been denied or was denied for a significant number of days, it was not due to damage at the premises or vicinity in most instances. It was a national or state lockdown! Non-damage denial of access extension can certainly play the trick here for specific organisations which were closed following Covid-19 incidents at their premises. The issue of evidence mentioned earlier would still be significant here.

4) **Act of Competent Authority:** National and state lockdowns

were declared by the president and respective governors as a response to the Covid-19 pandemic. Businesses were forced by this act of competent authority to shut down and individuals were mandated to stay at home. Again most policies in Nigeria does not provide coverage for this sort of situation. Non-damage denial of access is generally provided for prevention of access flowing from a thing in the premises or vicinity. Such "thing" is typically defined as disturbance, commotion, danger or damage. The loss must flow from the thing. This sort of actions is usually specific and not of a general nature like a national or statewide lockdown. These are areas of clarity which must come out of this crises. Again, without prejudice to what the courts might decide, insurers and reinsurers will have to be clear in their mind going forward on what is covered or not.

5) **Suppliers and Customers Extension:** Damage is usually required at the supplier or customers premises for this aspect of the policy to be triggered. The constraints highlighted above might apply here as well. We must note however that a new branch of business interruption policy has evolved from this extension (Contingent Business Interruption and Supply Chain). This new policy as highlighted in earlier chapters is more specific and clear in their wordings. Pandemics requiring quarantine are covered.

This area is certainly unfolding and emerging. Events in the next couple of months will provide clarity which will guide the conducts of the market going forward. We are trusting the competence of the courts to provide clarity on the existing wordings whilst we embrace the future which starts now.

## 8.2 A FEW DECIDED CASES

A number of cases have already gone to court and whilst a few cases have been decided as at August 2020, there are clear indications that these cases will go to appeal. A few cases have been summarised below. Readers are encouraged to keep tap of further appeals and other cases which will certainly come up.

### 1) A South African Case (A triump of Notifiable Disease Extension)

*Café Chameleon CC Vs Guardrisk Insurance Company Ltd (2020).* Café Chameleon launched an urgent application seeking a declaratory order that Guardrisk, a non-life insurer, is obliged to indemnify it, as policyholder, in terms of a Business Interruption clause in the insurance policy between the parties. Café Chameleon contended that it suffered losses as a result of the interruption caused by the Covid-19 pandemic and the subsequent nationwide lockdown imposed by the Regulations under the Disaster Management Act, 2002 (DMA Regulations). Café Chameleon lodged its claim under the Notifiable Diseases Extension clause in terms of the insurance policy, which provided business interruption cover for 'a notifiable disease occurring within a radius of 50km of the premises'. A notifiable disease is defined in the policy as, 'illness sustained by any person resulting from any human infectious or human contagious disease, an outbreak of which the competent local authority has stipulated shall be notified to them, but excluding HIV, AIDS or an AIDS related condition'. Café Chameleon also contended that as a result of the restricted movement and shut down of various businesses in terms of the DMA Regulations it sustained significant financial losses as it could not trade or receive customers during the lockdown period, being a restaurant. Although the DMA Regulations were progressively relaxed to allow for the preparation and delivery of prepared food, as Café Chameleon is primarily a sit-down restaurant, income generated from food deliveries in the past only amounted to 5% of the restaurant's turnover.

Guardrisk denied liability on the basis that the loss suffered by Café Chameleon was not covered under the Notifiable Diseases Extension clause in the insurance policy because the direct cause was the lockdown imposed by the DMA Regulations and not the Covid-19 pandemic. In other words, Guardrisk argued that there was no causal connection between the lockdown and the Notifiable Diseases Extension. The Court disagreed with Guardrisk and held that the insurance policy must be interpreted so its provisions receive fair and sensible application having regard to the context and to ensure a business-like or commercially sound result. The Court further held that the policy cannot be interpreted with reference to other policies or based on generalised concerns about the impact of Covid-19 on the insurance industry at large. Regarding whether Covid-19 falls within the Notifiable Disease Extension of the Policy, the Court held that it does. The Court found that although Covid-19 was determined as a notifiable disease by national government and not a local authority is irrelevant. The Court also considered the issue of causation. The Court looked at factual causation and applied the but for test to hold that there is a clear nexus between the Covid-19 outbreak and the DMA Regulations, which caused interruption to the business of Café Chameleon. On the question of legal causation, the Court held that the harm is not too remote from the peril and that it is fair, reasonable and just to burden Guardrisk with liability. The Court also found that, the argument of opening the floodgates of liability cannot stand because each case will be decided upon its own facts, policy wording and the law. The Court issued a declaratory order to the effect that the Guardrisk is liable to indemnify Café Chameleon in terms of the Business Interruption clause contained in the insurance policy between the parties.

## 2) An American Case (Physical Loss of Damage is required)

*Gavrilides Management Company, et al. Vs Michigan Ins. Co (2020)*

On July 1, 2020, Judge Joyce Draganchuk in Ingham County, Michigan dismissed a claim of first impression, siding with an insurer's decision to deny business interruption coverage. The case centered on one key provision in the insured's policy: "Direct physical loss of or damage to the [insured's] property" triggers the application of business interruption coverage. Nick Gavrilides is the owner of two restaurants in Lansing, Michigan. His insurer Michigan Insurance, a subsidiary of Donegal Group Inc., denied his $650,000.00 claim. Gavrilides' asserted his business interruption coverage should include Covid-19-related losses. Michigan Insurance argued the policy did not cover losses stemming from Covid-19. It argued business interruption coverage is triggered by an event that actually alters the structural integrity of the property, which did not occur. Gavrilides, on the other hand, argued non-destructive losses are covered by the policy. Gavrilides did not allege his property had been damaged or lost but instead that Michigan Governor Gretchen Whitmer's stay-at-home order interfered with his use of his restaurant business. In response, Michigan Insurance pointed out the policy was not triggered by loss of use of the property but rather by the loss of or damage to the physical property itself. The insurer maintained, "The insured's property today exists in the very same condition as it existed the day prior to the effective date of the stay-at-home order."

The Michigan court agreed. Judge Draganchuk ruled verbally during the hearing: *"It is clear from the policy coverage that only direct physical loss is covered. Under their common meanings and under federal case law ... direct physical loss of or damage to the property has to be something with material existence, something that is tangible, ... something that alters the physical integrity of the property. The Complaint here does not allege any physical loss of or damage to the property."*

In other words, the court ruled that Michigan Insurance's denial of Gavrilides' claim was proper because Covid-19 did not affect the actual, tangible structure of his restaurants, and as such, there was no physical loss of, or damage to, the restaurants. Similarly, Judge Draganchuk also dismissed Gavrilides' claim for coverage pursuant to the civil authority provision in the policy, because this provision also requires the physical loss or damage to trigger coverage. The final nail in the claim's coffin was a virus exclusion contained in the policy, which stated the insurer "will not pay for loss or damages caused by or resulting from any virus, bacterium, or other microorganism that induces or is capable of inducing physical distress, illness, or disease."

### 3) The UK Example (Non-Damage BI and Regulatory Clarity)

The United Kingdom's Financial Conduct Authority (FCA) which regulates insurance business decided to seek clarity from the court by instituting a test case on behalf of SMEs. The hearings were concluded in July 2020 and judgement is expected in September 2020. If the court's decision supports the FCA then insurers with business interruption exposure in the United Kingdom could experience a significant increase in pandemic-related losses. The test case is expected to be persuasive for other common law jurisdictions currently considering business interruption cases of their own including Nigeria.

The two main issues in contention in the test case are as follows:

**Coverage**: Whether the non-damage business interruption policies under their terms cover losses resulting from the coronavirus pandemic.

**Causation**: Whether, as a matter of law and fact and in light of the business interruption policies themselves, the necessary causal link is established between the assumed losses and the relevant peril, event or circumstance that is covered, including the impact, if any, of any trends clause.

The other issues raised in the test case relates to the parties' knowledge, interpretation of individual terms, public authority orders and prohibitions, prevention or hindrance of access or use of premises, vicinity, prevalence of disease, trend clause.

The test case raises a range of issues which are of great significance to the operation of business interruption policies. The disputes in relation to the appropriate approach to causation and the proper interpretation of insurance policies mean that the court's decision could be a landmark. Most likely this case like many others will go to the highest level of appeal. Whatever, the outcome may be, it is certain that the understanding and practice of business interruption insurance will change for ever.

# BIBLIOGRAPHY

**Allan Manning and Steven Manning (2013).** *Mannings Guide to Interruption Insurance.* Melbourne. LMI Group.

**Aon Claim Preparation Manual (2010).** www.aon.com

**Bayo Samagbeyi (2019).** *Advance Business Interruption Insurance.* Lecture Notes. Lagos. FASCON.

**Caroline Woolley (2010).** *Contingent Business Interruption (non-damage) and Supply Chain Risk.* Mumbai. Marsh.

**Damian Glynn (2005).** *Beware Cover Issues –Business Interruption.* Essex. The Garda Solution.

**Damian Glynn (2020).** *Coronavirus: BI issues.* Chartered Insurance Institute. Webinar presented on 3rd April 2020.

**Damian Glynn, Sue Taylor and Steven Nock (2020).** *The Basic Business Interruption Book.* Scotland. Witherby

**Diane Jenkins, London Business Interruption Association (2016).** *Business Interruption Insurance.* https://www.cii.co.uk/knowledge/resources/articles/business-interruption-insurance/7051

**Gordon JR Hickmott (1999).** *Interruption insurance: practical issues.* London. Witherby.

**Hanna Schieve (2018).** *NDBI: the missing piece of your business interruption insurance.* Online article. https://www.insurancebusinessmag.com/us/risk-management/operational/ndbi-the-missing-piece-of-your-business-interruption-insurance-91533.aspx. July 2, 2019.

**Harry Roberts (2016).** *Riley on business interruption insurance.* 10th edition. London: Sweet and Maxwell.

**Insurance Institute of London (2019).** *Business Interruption Policy Wordings – Challenges Highlighted by Claims Experience.* London. Insurance Institute of London and Chartered Institute of Loss Adjusters.

**Jill Cranston Rice (2020).** *The First COVID-19 Business Interruption Decision Sides In Favor of Insurers.* Online article. https://www.natlawreview.com/article/first-covid-19-business-interruption-decision-sides-favor-insurers_July 15, 2020

**Keryn Layton-Mccann,Christine Rodrigues (2020).** *Covid-19: High Court Decision On Business Interruption Insurance Claim.* Online article. https://www.bowmanslaw.com/insights/banking-and-financial-services-regulatory/covid-19-high-court-decision-on-business-interruption-insurance-claim/ July 8, 2020.

**London Business Interruption Association (2010).** *Guide to Business Interruption Insurance and Claims.* London. LBIA

**Lon A. Berk and Michael S. Levine (2013).** *Contingent Business Interruption Coverage for Superstorm Sandy Losses.* American Bar Association Section of Litigation – Insurance Coverage. February 26, 2013

**Swiss Re (2004).** *Business Interruption Insurance.* Zurich

**Insurance Information Institute (2020).** *Protecting your business against contingent business interruption and supply chain disruption.* http://www.iii.org/article/protecting-your-business-against-contingent-business-interruption-and-supply-chain-disruption

## ABOUT THE AUTHOR

Peter Offiong has over a decade of post-professional insurance qualification experience. He became an Associate of the Chartered Insurance Institute of Nigeria in 2009 (AIIN). He is also a chartered accountant and associate of the Institute of Chartered Accountants of Nigeria (ACA). Peter is an associate of the Nigerian Council of Registered Insurance Brokers as well as Nigerian Institute of Management.

He holds a BSc in Business Management and MSc in Finance from the University of Calabar and Lead City University respectively. He has lectured students preparing for the professional examinations of the Chartered Insurance Institute of Nigeria since 2010 whilst also contributing to various technical and insurance industry journals. He is an executive member of the Offices Representatives Committee (ORC) of the Chartered Insurance Institute of Nigeria where he also heads the Workshop Committee. Peter has handled and supported various business interruption claims.

He currently heads the Financial & Professional Service unit at Scib Nigeria & Co. Ltd, the leading insurance broking firm in Nigeria.

www.ingramcontent.com/pod-product-compliance
Lightning Source LLC
Chambersburg PA
CBHW060844220526
45466CB00003B/1236